Leslie's Lane The Book!

D1571236

Contents

*A lane is a path that is clearly defined. And it directly
moves you from one place to the next. Leslie's Lane
should be a GLOBAL catalyst in its purpose and literally
be able to take you on that spiritual, informational,
and physical journey from point A to point B.*

—P. NIGEL KILLIKELLY

Introduction

Greetings, Beautiful Friends! ☺

How are you? I trust that you are having a great day! Leslie's Lane evolved in two ways. Firstly, as a writer of more than twenty years on subjects that range from business, careers, and consumer finance to lifestyle, health, travel, and religion, I have been able to amass a wealth of knowledge through my interaction with some of the world's most renowned experts in their field of study.

I found that in seeing my articles in wonderful publications like *The Atlanta Bulletin, CrossRoadsNews, Atlanta Parent, Say Amen, Good News, UPSCALE, Black Enterprise, eHow, Chron.com, ESSENCE, FORTUNE, WSJ/ Dow Jones Newswires*, and more, my family and friends frequently reached out to me. They called to request my assistance with information and resources important to their daily lives. Although the people requesting info were different from one another, all of them shared a common thread of wanting to know basically the same thing(s).

I received queries like, "How do I save on and find places to travel? How do I find resources on scholarships, and medical and dental insurance? How do I find coupons to get discounts on eating out at restaurants? How do I get the free stuff you talk about in articles?"

Secondly, my wonderful husband, Tony, is the former Owner/Operator of Chick-fil-A Turner Hill Road—"Home of the 1,000th Chick-fil-A." For the last fifteen years, I've had many people ask me about employment with him.

I feel like everyone who wants a job ought to have one. Moreover, I feel like everyone should be able to have the career he or she loves.

Therefore, more than five years ago, I set about e-mailing a list of information on jobs, discounts, resources, and free stuff. Not too much later, I created a blog and called it Leslie's Lane, a consumer information blog on jobs, discounts, travel, resources, scholarships, and free stuff. I love FREE STUFF!!!!

I could say "the rest is history." But isn't that so cliché? I'll just say that Leslie's Lane has evolved beyond my wildest dreams and imagination! So many people tell me how helpful it is, and they pass it on to everyone they know! I love that because I designed it to be educational, informational, inspirational, motivational, and empowering. I guess it was just a matter of time before I wrote *Leslie's Lane The Book!* This is the first volume in The Leslie's Lane Series.

Remember the times that you (or your parents) didn't have the Internet? You called a family member or friend on the phone and talked about what you needed. I wanted this book to be conversational in that way, just as Leslie's Lane blog is conversational. This book is unique, but then, that's me! At the beginning of each chapter, it mirrors the typical Leslie's Lane posts—complete with salutations and a smiley face emoji. I've grown accustomed to doing that! It was important to me for this book to not only inform and educate, but also serve as a catalyst to enhance and change the lives of others. As such, at the end of each chapter, I have made it interactive.

You and I are sort of partners in my first Leslie's Lane book! So feel free to answer questions, fill in the blanks, read between the lines, write outside of the lines—whatever you want to do! I trust that this book is helpful to you, your family, and friends. Feel free to pass the word on about *Leslie's Lane The Book!* as well as check out my Leslie's Lane website at www.LesliesLane.com and blog at www.LesliesLane.wordpress.com; like my Facebook page, Leslie's Lane, and follow me on Twitter and Instagram @LesliesLane. Thanks so much for your support, and have a great week! Happy Reading and Research!

Sincerely,

Leslie E. Royal

I Dedicate This Book to My Beautiful Family!

*To my wonderful husband, Tony, daughter, Antasha, and son, Jay
You all are truly the wind beneath my wings! Thank you so much for your love
and unwavering support as well as being a blessing to me! I love you!*

#TheRoyalFamilyMagic
"A Picture of Love, Joy & Happiness"

One

JOBS

Greetings, Beautiful Friends! ☺

As I shared in the intro, I feel like everyone who wants a job ought to have one. The wealth of information in this first chapter should help point you in the right direction as you seek employment.

It doesn't matter whether you are a teen, adult, or senior. You can find information on employment here. Just think about whether you want to work part time, full time, weekends, seasonally, or be a stay-at-home mom or stay-at-home dad. Are you looking for advancement within your own organization or would you like a whole new career?

I want to add a little anecdote here. My daughter, Antasha, was eight years old at the time. She asked me what she was going to be when she grew up. And I gave her the answer any good mom would. I said, "You can be whatever you want to be!"

But that was an inauthentic answer because I wasn't what I wanted to be. I wasn't the best I could be! I had a good job with benefits as a clerk at the FBI. But my love and passion was and is writing. I was on the newspaper staff from seventh grade to twelfth grade. My undergrad degree is in Journalism. After the conversation with my daughter and my epiphany, I immediately set out on my dream! For two years, I continued to work full time while writing for local publications. When I could afford to do so, I resigned. Word of advice: follow your dreams. But don't quit your day job too quickly!

Please feel free to check out all links to jobs whether in the states or internationally. You might want to work in civil service like I did. Check out FBI, CIA, Secret Service, and other links I have included in this chapter. There are so many career options! Just meditate on what's best for you! At the end of the chapter, please check out questions that might be of interest to you. Thanks so much for your support, and have a great week! Happy Reading and Research!

Sincerely,

Leslie

Can you tell me about jobs?

"I think an ideal job environment should be one where each employee, from the newest employee to the general manager, CEO, and president, embodies and practices the morals, values, standards and vision of the company daily. Can you tell me about this type environment? What are some good company perks and benefits? How do pay rates get determined for specific job positions? Whenever a large company or corporation hires from within, what is it that internal employees can do to make themselves stand out?"

— Sigi Cayel, a millennial
ready to make her mark on the world,
is a meeting and special events coordinator for a luxury hotel.

Perspective & Words of Advice
from *Leslie's Lane: The Book!*
Jobs Expert

"To make yourself stand out in your company, focus on the mental, emotional, physical and spiritual. Be a student. Have an insatiable appetite to grow in knowledge and understanding. Have intellectual curiosity. Secondly, be passionate about your work and career. There are so many tremendous online resources now. Redesign your role. In doing so, it makes you excited about your work. Thirdly, keep yourself in shape physically. God put this mind and heart in a physical body, and it has to be maintained. Like a car or truck, it has to have regularly scheduled and preventive maintenance. Be disciplined about what we eat and the exercise that we get to keep our minds sharp and attentive. Fourth area, regardless of any religious perspective, is that we have to protect and guard our hearts from a spiritual standpoint. The spiritual part—which is often overlooked—is the heart and soul of mission and purpose. Regarding salary, it is all scaled to your acumen, preparation and educational level and aspirations. We all live in a competitive environment. It works to our advantage to give ourselves as much of a competitive advantage as possible. In terms of overall perks and benefits for our corporate staff, at no charge, we provide breakfast, lunch, a fitness center, nutritionists and personal trainers. We have a daycare center on campus with childcare that is far below market rate as well as both insurance and retirement plans. As you add it all up, the part of the biggest benefit is "The Three C's"—competence, character and chemistry—of the workforce and individuals that work with us. We try to create an environment where people can do their best work. I call it the sandbox. Where you just want to play and play. Have your most fun time with people that you want to work with doing purposeful and meaningful work. People really line up with our corporate purpose—realizing we are a different society and culture by having a strong, robust brand that creates employment and satisfies our customers. But we do so with the idea in mind that we are being a positive influence on all who come in contact with Chick-fil-A. My father said, "Fall in love with your work and you never have to work again."

— Dan T. Cathy is the Chairman and Chief Executive Officer (CEO) of Chick-fil-A, Inc.

Leslie's Lessons—Five Tips at a Glance! Check Out Some of the Best Job Websites

1. www.indeed.com
2. www.monster.com
3. www.careerbuilder.com
4. www.job.com
5. www.snagajob.com

Leslie's Litany—Three Books to Read! Check Out Some of the Best Job Books

1. *The Leap: Launching Your Full-Time Career in Our Part-Time Economy* by Robert Dickie
2. *What Color is Your Parachute?* by Richard N. Bolles
3. *Knock 'em Dead: The Ultimate Job Search Guide* by Martin Yate, CPC

Leslie's Lane The Book!
Expert Info at a Glance!
Company: Chick-fil-A, Inc.
Website: http://www.chick-fil-a.com/
Facebook: https://www.facebook.com/ChickfilAIncHeadquarters/
Twitter: @ChickfilA and @dancathy
Instagram: @chickfila and @dancathy

As you begin the job search, consider whether you would like to work full time, part time, weekends, seasonally, and so forth. Create a professional resume. To save money, you can ask a friend or relative proficient in writing to help you. Nowadays, websites and job-search engines can help you create an excellent resume and offer free advice on the job hunt. Check out these sites:
www.resume-now.com/FreeResume
myperfectresume.com/Free/ResumeBuilder
www.resumehelp.com
www.super-resume.com/
https://www.gotresumebuilder.com/

As best you can, match your experience, education, and yes...your passion... with your job interest. The best job sites on the following pages are more than enough to get you started. Plus, you can order popular books to help you. In the meantime, let's check out some of my favorite sites, corporations, and organizations.

Chick-fil-A Corporate Careers—Would you like to work for the best company in the world? OK...I might be a little partial! As I shared, my husband Tony was a Chick-fil-A Owner/Operator! I absolutely love Chick-fil-A and every-thing it represents! There are many other great companies in the United States and throughout the world. Please check out my Leslie's Labor 500 list of great companies! But in the meantime, please check out this link to Chick-fil-A corporate careers, and if you're interested, franchised operator opportunities.
http://www.chick-fil-a.com/Company/Careers-Guide

I'm singling out Uber and Lyft because they are some of the hottest gigs going! You can make your own schedule. You can work part time or full time. You can work night or day. You can take off weekends if you care to do so.
Make $35 an hour driving for Lyft:
https://www.lyft.com/
Make money with Uber as a driver!
https://www.uber.com/

I worked for the FBI for ten years. The federal government takes really good care of its employees, and I enjoyed really good benefits. Check out their websites to see if employment with them would work for you.

Careers with the FBI:

https://www.fbijobs.gov/

Careers with the CIA:

https://www.cia.gov/careers

Careers with the Secret Service:

http://www.secretservice.gov/join/careers/

Careers with the federal government:

https://www.usajobs.gov/

The US Postal Service is an independent agency. If you are interested in a career with them, please click on this link to check it out:

https://about.usps.com/careers/welcome.htm

My children, Antasha and Jay, both began working at my husband's Chick-fil-A restaurant at the age of fourteen. Yes! Mental note! Chick-fil-A hires at fourteen! If you're like me, you're glad to keep your kids busy and allow them to earn extra money for clothes, school needs, and other expenses. If you know of a teen looking for employment, the following websites would be a great start for them:

www.snagajob.com

www.groovejob.com

www.hireteen.com

Tony and I always felt it is vitally important to reinvest in the community he serves. In addition to the Chick-fil-A Corporation, I went in search of companies that make it a point to serve their communities well. I found these sites. I pulled out three to get you started.

Fifty Most Civic-Minded Companies—http://www.civic50.org/2014-results.php

General Mills Careers—http://careers.generalmills.com/?country=united-states

The Hershey Company Careers—https://www.thehersheycompany.com/careers.aspx
Western Union Careers—http://careers.westernunion.com/

I think it's important to find excitement and meaning in one's job. Working at a technology company doesn't have to be a mundane job. It can be really exciting, interesting, and enjoyable. Check out a few of the most exciting jobs for techies!
Twitter—https://about.twitter.com/careers
Google—https://www.google.com/about/careers/
Riverbed—http://www.riverbed.com/about/careers/

Get paid to work from home! Many reputable jobs are available compliments of my hero—Clark Howard! I've been following consumer advocate Clark Howard for many years. I am a big fan of his. I like everything he discusses. I particularly like his section on reputable at-home work opportunities. We often see advertisements of at-home jobs making thousands of dollars. But Clark gives insight on legitimate stay-at-home gigs at http://www.clarkhoward.com/legitimate-work-from-home-opportunities.
Another work from home site is Rat Race Rebellion. Check out their site. http://ratracerebellion.com/

Mystery shopping organizations offer really great gigs! I know from personal experience! I really liked doing mystery shopping, but my writing allowed little time for it. What I love about mystery shopping is that you get paid to do things that you would do anyway! You have to go to get grocery, to the gas station, take your pet to the vet, and like to go out to dinner! You get paid to do that! Please click on the links below to sign up with these organizations. But before you do, check out this link to an article that I wrote for *Black Enterprise* back in the day, "Get Paid to Shop," at
http://black-enterprise.vlex.com/vid/get-paid-to-shop-54361191!

www.nationalassociationofmysteryshoppers.org/
www.mysteryshoppers.com

www.secretshoppers.com
www.secretshopping.com
www.mysteryshop.org/
http://aamerch.com/
http://www.a-closer-look.com/
https://shopperhub.second-to-none.com/login.aspx?ReturnUrl=%2f
https://www.sassieshop.com/sassie/SassieShopperSignup/Signup.
php?EmsID=myrB8l%2FCMJY%3D
http://www.spiesindisguise.com/secure/login.asp

Get paid to test all sorts of awesome new products! The only thing I would like more than getting stuff for free is getting paid to test the free stuff. I've never had the opportunity, but I would love to do so. If this is of interest to you, check out a few links with info on companies offering this cool gig:
www.productreviewmom.com
http://moneypantry.com/product-testing/

There are lots of job websites or search engines out there. I think that these are ten of the best:

1. www.indeed.com
2. www.monster.com
3. www.careerbuilder.com
4. www.job.com
5. www.snagajob.com
6. www.simplyhired.com
7. www.usajobs.com
8. www.idealist.org
9. www.theladders.com
10. www.glassdoor.com

How can prospective employees do great in an interview? I queried Dan on this subject and was so impressed by the profound responses, I had to share this entire section with you!

A Must-Read Questionnaire EXCLUSIVELY for *Leslie's Lane The Book!* By Dan T. Cathy

One of the objectives is to be unique and distinguish yourself. I find in an interview setting, oftentimes, the prospective employer is sitting there asking all the questions while the prospective applicants just try their best to summarize their response to those questions. And that's very typical. However, for employees to distinguish themselves, they really ought to switch or turn the tables. They ought to be the ones asking all the questions of the employer. They should have in their mind that they are special and unique, and this employer will be very lucky to get them. So what's the employer doing to earn the opportunity to work with a particular individual? So I will be asking questions along the lines of:

1. What is the atmosphere going to be here?
2. How supportive are you as an employer to new ideas, creativity and problem solving?

3. How ready are you to reward and recognize outstanding performance?
4. What type of commitment do you have to continuing education and for me to continue to develop myself educationally?
5. What books and tuition assistance, workshops, or other kinds of things are you going to make available to me while I am here with you to grow and develop myself?

As an employer, those kinds of questions from a prospective employee get my attention really, really quick. That means that as an employer, I'm going to have to bring my "A-game." This will not be business as usual. This is an employee who's going to, in all likelihood, create tremendous value for my organization. I better be willing to pay this person what he or she is worth because this employee is going to be in high demand and short supply.

Dan, Chairman and CEO of Chick-fil-A, is the son of legendary founder S. Truett Cathy. It was an honor for Tony and me to have known Truett. He was the kindest man in the world! As for Dan, I have found him to be a kind, generous and supportive friend! If it's important to his friends, family and Chick-fil-A operators, staff, families and guests, it's important to Dan!!!!!

**Use the FREE space below to freestyle!
Grab some colored pencils and doodle, draw, brainstorm, reflect or whatever!**

Leslie's Labor 500

Employment in up-and-coming companies is included. Leslie's Labor 500 includes some of the best companies in the world! Listed in alphabetical order, check out their sites for employment! If you find the links are no longer available, feel free to Google the company's name and enter "careers" or "jobs."

1. Aaron's Inc.—https://jobs.aarons.com/
2. AARP—http://www.aarp.org/about-aarp/careers/
3. Acacia Communications—http://acacia-inc.com/careers/
4. Accenture—https://www.accenture.com/us-en/careers
5. Accor Hotels—http://www.accorhotels-group.com/en/recruitment-and-careers.html
6. Acer—http://www.acer.com/ac/en/US/content/careers
7. Activision Blizzard—http://www.activisionblizzard.com/careers
8. Acuity—http://www.acuitybrands.com/about-us/careers
9. AdColony—http://www.adcolony.com/team-and-careers/
10. Adidas—https://careers.adidas-group.com/jobs
11. Adobe—http://www.adobe.com/careers.html
12. Aetna—http://aetna.jobs/
13. AGCO Corp—https://careers.agcocorp.com/
14. Aldo—http://www.aldogroup.com/career-opportunities.html
15. Alex and Ani—https://www.alexandani.com/careers
16. Allegis Group—https://www.allegisgroup.com/careers
17. Allianz Life Insurance—https://www.allianzlife.com/about/careers
18. AllState—https://www.allstate.com/careers.aspx
19. Alston & Byrd—http://www.alston.com/alstoncareers/
20. Amazon—https://www.amazon.jobs/
21. American Airlines—http://careers.aa.com/en/ac/home
22. American Family Insurance—https://www.amfam.com/about/careers
23. American Solar—https://www.americansolardirect.com/careers/
24. American Wireless—http://www.americanwireless.us/careers.html
25. Apple—http://www.apple.com/jobs/us/
26. Arby's—http://arbys.com/careers

27. ARI (Automotive Resources International)—http://www.arifleet. com/about/careers/
28. Armani—http://www.armanicareers.com/en
29. Arnold & Porter LLP—http://www.arnoldporter.com/en/careers
30. Arris Group Inc.—http://www.arris.com/Careers
31. Asbury Automotive Group Inc.—http://www.asburycareers.com/
32. Asics—http://www.asics.com/us/en-us/careers
33. Assurant—https://jobs.assurant.com/
34. Asus—http://www.asus.com/US/ASUS-Employment/ careers-at-asus/
35. Atlantic Health System—http://www.atlantichealth.org/atlantic/ careers/careers
36. Auto Desk Inc.—http://jobs.autodesk.com/
37. AutoTrader—http://careers.autotrader.com/
38. Avery Dennison—http://www.averydennison.com/en/home/careers. html
39. Avon—http://careers.avoncompany-northamerica.com/
40. Axiall Corp—http://www.axiall.com/Careers/
41. Bain—http://www.bain.com/careers/
42. Baker Donelson—http://www.bakerdonelson.com/careers/
43. Bank of America—http://careers.bankofamerica.com/search-jobs. aspx?c=united-states&r=us
44. Barclays Bank—https://www.home.barclays/careers.html
45. Barnes & Noble—http://www.barnesandnoble.com/h/careers
46. Baskin Robbins—https://www.baskinrobbins.com/content/ baskinrobbins/en/careers.html
47. Bath and Body Works—http://careers.lb.com/working-here/ bath-body-works
48. Bayer Nordic—https://career.nordic.bayer.com/en/
49. BCBG Max Azria—http://www.bcbgmaxazriagroup.com/careers/
50. Bed, Bath and Beyond—http://www.bedbathandbeyond.com/ store/static/Careers

51. Berkshire Hathaway—https://www.bhhc.com/careers/current-openings.aspx
52. Best Buy—http://careers.bestbuy.ca/csbsites/bestbuy/searchresults.asp
53. Best Western Hotels & Resorts—http://www.bestwestern.com/about-us/careers/
54. Big Boy Restaurant & Bakery/Frisch's Big Boy—http://www.frischs.com/careers/careers.aspx
55. Bimbo Bakeries USA—https://careers.bimbobakeriesusa.com/
56. Birkenstock—https://www.birkenstockusa.com/about/careers
57. Blue Bottle Coffee—https://bluebottlecoffee.com/careers
58. Blue Cross Blue Shield—http://www.bcbs.com/careers/
59. BlueLinx Holdings Inc.—http://bluelinxco.com/careers.aspx
60. Bob Evans Restaurants—http://employment.bobevans.com/
61. Bodhtree Solutions—http://www.bodhtree.com/careers.php
62. Boeing—http://www.boeing.com/careers/
63. Bojangles' Famous Chicken 'n Biscuits—https://www.bojangles.com/careers/
64. Bonefish Grill—https://www.bonefishgrill.com/careers
65. Books-a-Million—http://www.booksamillioninc.com/careers.html
66. Bosch—https://www.bosch-career.us/en/
67. Boston Consulting Group—http://www.bcg.com/careers/default.aspx
68. Boston Market—http://bostonmarketjobs.com/
69. BP—http://www.bp.com/en/global/bp-careers.html
70. Brinks—https://www.brinks.com/en/careers
71. Brooks—http://www.brooksrunning.com/en_us/meet-brooks/careers
72. Buffalo Wild Wings—http://www.buffalowildwings.com/en/careers/
73. Build Group Construction—http://www.buildgc.com/groundup/careers/
74. Burberry—https://burberrycareers.com/

75. Burger King—https://www.bk.com/careers/
76. Burns & McDonnell—http://www.burnsmcd.com/careers
77. Buy PD—https://buypd.com/jobs/
78. C. D. Moody Construction—http://www.cdmoodyconstruction.com/?page_id=55
79. Cadence—http://cadence.jobs/
80. California Pizza Kitchen—http://www.cpk.com/Career
81. Camden Property Trust—https://www.camdenliving.com/careers
82. Campbell Soup—http://careers.campbellsoupcompany.com/
83. Capitol One—https://jobs.capitalone.com/
84. Car Max Inc.—http://jobs.carmax.com/
85. Cargill Inc.—http://www.cargill.com/careers/
86. Caribou Coffee—http://www.cariboucoffeejobs.com/
87. Carl's Jr.—http://www.carlsjr.com/jobs
88. Carlson Rezidor Hotel Group—http://carlsonrezidor.com/careers
89. Carrabba's Italian Grill—https://www.carrabbas.com/careers
90. Carter's Inc.—http://corporate.carters.com/corporateCareers.html
91. CCCi—https://www.ctcommunitycare.org/careers/
92. CDW—http://www.cdwjobs.com/
93. Centennial Lending Group—http://www.clg-llc.com/join-our-team/
94. Cheddars—http://cheddars.com/join-our-team/
95. Cheesecake Factory—http://jobs.thecheesecakefactory.com/
96. Chevron—http://careers.chevron.com/
97. CHG Healthcare Services—http://www.chghealthcare.com/careers/
98. Chick-fil-A—http://www.chick-fil-a.com/Company/Careers-Guide
99. Chili's Grill and Bar—http://www.chilisjobs.com/
100. Chipotle Mexican Grill & Bar—https://careers.chipotle.com/
101. Chiquita Brands—http://www.chiquita.com/Careers.aspx
102. Choice Hotels—http://careers.choicehotels.com/careers.html
103. Chuck E. Cheese's—https://www.chuckecheese.com/careers
104. Church's Chicken—http://www.churchs.com/careers.php

105. Cici's Pizza—https://www.cicis.com/careers
106. Cigna—http://www.cigna.com/careers/
107. Circle K—http://www.circlek.com/job-board?language=en
108. Cisco Systems—https://jobs.cisco.com/
109. Citgo—https://www.citgo.com/Careers.jsp
110. Citrix—https://jobs.citrix.com/
111. Claire's—http://clairescareers.com/
112. Clarks—https://am.clarksjobs.com/join-us/vacancies/
113. Clearleap—http://clearleap.com/company/careers/
114. Clif Bar—http://www.clifbar.com/careers
115. Cloud Sherpas—http://cloudsherpascareers.force.com/careers
116. Coach—http://www.coach.com/careers-about-coach.html
117. Colgate Palmolive—https://jobs.colgate.com/
118. Comcast—http://jobs.comcast.com/
119. Compaq—http://www8.hp.com/us/en/jobs/index.html
120. Con Agra Foods—http://www.conagrafoodscareers.com/
121. Connexion Point—https://www.connexionpoint.com/careers.php
122. Conoco—http://conocophillips.site.findly.com/
123. Constellation Brands—http://www.cbrands.com/careers
124. Converse—https://www.converse.com/uk/en/about-careers/Careers-About-Us.html
125. Cooley LLP—https://www.cooley.com/careers.aspx
126. Costco—http://www.costco.com/jobs.html
127. Cracker Barrel Old Country Store—https://www.crackerbarrel.com/careers
128. Credit Acceptance Corporation—https://www.creditacceptance.com/careers
129. Crescendo Bioscience—https://crescendobio.com/company/careers/
130. Culver's—http://www.culvers.com/careers
131. Custom Ink LLC—http://www.customink.com/about/jobs/
132. Dairy Farmers of America—http://www.dfamilk.com/careers
133. Dairy Queen—http://www.dairyqueen.com/us-en/Company/Careers/?localechange=1&

134. Dannon Co.—http://somethingspecialinside.com/Index.aspx
135. Datto—http://www.datto.com/careers
136. David Weekly Homes—http://workforweekley.com/
137. Dean Foods—http://www.deanfoods.com/our-company/careers.aspx
138. Dell—http://www.dell.com/learn/us/en/uscorp1/careers/dell-career-and-job-landing-page?c=us&l=en&s=corp
139. Delta Airlines—https://delta.greatjob.net/jobs/EntryServlet
140. Deloitte—http://www2.deloitte.com/us/en/pages/careers/topics/careers.html
141. Denny's—https://www.dennys.com/careers/
142. Devon Energy—https://careers.devonenergy.com/
143. Dicks Sporting Goods—http://www.dickssportinggoods.jobs/
144. DirecTV—http://att.jobs/careers
145. Dish Network—http://careers.dish.com/
146. DKNY—https://www.dkny.com/careers.html
147. Dolce & Gabbana—http://www.dolcegabbana.com/corporate/en/job_en.html
148. Dole Food Company, Inc.—http://www.dole.com/AboutDole/Careers
149. Domino's Pizza—https://jobs.dominos.com/dominos-careers/
150. Dooney & Burke—https://www.dooney.com/careers.html
151. Dr Pepper Snapple—http://www.drpeppersnapplegroup.com/careers/
152. Drury Hotels—http://www.drurycareers.com/
153. Dynamic Dental Partners—http://ddpgroups.atsondemand.com/
154. ECHO Health CenseoHealth—https://www.censeohealth.com/careers
155. Edible Arrangements—https://www.ediblearrangements.com/edible-careers/edible-arrangements-careers
156. Edelman—http://www.edelman.com/careers-and-culture/jobs/
157. Edward Jones—http://careers.edwardjones.com/index.html
158. El Pollo Loco—https://www.elpolloloco.com/careers/
159. Electrolux—http://www.electroluxgroup.com/en/category/career/

160. Esprit—http://www.esprit.com/careers
161. Exide Technologies Inc.—http://www.exide.com/us/en/careers.aspx
162. Exxon—http://corporate.exxonmobil.com/en/company/careers
163. Facebook—https://www.facebook.com/careers/
164. Fact Set Research Systems—http://www.factset.com/careers
165. Fairmont Raffles Hotels—http://www.raffles.com/careers/
166. Famous Dave's—http://www.famousdaves.com/careers
167. First Data Corp.—https://www.firstdata.com/en_us/about-first-data/careers-home.html
168. First Point Power—http://www.firstpointpower.com/careers/index.html
169. Fitbit—https://www.fitbit.com/jobs
170. Five Guys Burgers—http://www.fiveguys.com/contact-us/careers
171. Flickr—https://www.flickr.com/jobs
172. Foot Locker—http://sneakerjobs.com/
173. Flowers Foods Inc.—http://www.flowersfoods.com/FFC_Careers/
174. Ford—http://corporate.ford.com/careers.html
175. Four Seasons Hotels & Resorts—http://jobs.fourseasons.com/
176. Fuhu—http://fuhu.mytribehr.com/careers
177. GE—http://www.ge.com/careers
178. Geico—https://www.geico.com/careers/opportunities/
179. General Electric—http://www.ge.com/careers
180. General Mills—http://careers.generalmills.com/
181. General Motors—http://careers.gm.com/
182. Genuine Parts Company—http://jobs.genpt.com/
183. Georgia Aquarium—http://www.georgiaaquarium.org/careers
184. GlassDoor.com—http://jobs.jobvite.com/glassdoor?id=GLASA001M
185. Global Payments Inc—https://www.globalpaymentsinc.com/us/company/careers/
186. GNC—http://careers.gnc.com/
187. Golden Corral—http://goldencorral.hodesiq.com/job_start.asp

188. Goldman Sachs Group—http://www.goldmansachs.com/careers/index.html
189. Google Inc.—https://www.google.com/intl/en/about/careers/
190. GoPro—https://gopro.com/careers
191. GovSmart—http://www.govsmart.com/career-opportunities/
192. Graphic Package Holdings—https://careers.graphicpkg.com/
193. Great Lakes Cheese—http://www.greatlakescheese.com/careers-great-lakes-cheese.aspx
194. Greenway Medical Technologies—https://www.greenwayhealth.com/careers/
195. H D Supply Holding—http://hdsupply.jobs/
196. H. J. Heinz Co—http://www.kraftheinzcompany.com/careers.html
197. Hardee's—http://www.hardees.com/jobs
198. Hasbro—https://jobs.hasbro.com/
199. Healthport—https://www.healthport.com/careers
200. Hershey Co.—https://careers.thehersheycompany.com/us/en/
201. Hewlett-Packard—http://h30631.www3.hp.com/
202. Hilcorp—http://www.hilcorp.com/
203. Hilti Inc.—https://careers.hilti.com/en
204. Hilton Worldwide—http://jobs.hiltonworldwide.com/select-country.php
205. Hormel Foods—https://www.hormelfoods.com/Careers/Careers.aspx
206. HSBC Bank—http://www.hsbc.com/careers
207. Hugo Boss—http://group.hugoboss.com/en/career/
208. Humana—https://www.humana.com/about/careers/
209. Hyatt Hotels—http://www.hyatt.jobs/
210. Hyland Software Inc.—https://www.onbase.com/en/about/careers
211. IBM—http://www-03.ibm.com/employment/
212. Icebreaker—http://eu.icebreaker.com/en/careers/careers.html
213. If(We)—Tagged, Hi5, NOD—http://www.ifwe.co/jobs/
214. IHOP—http://www.ihop.com/careers

215. In-N-Out Burger—http://www.in-n-out.com/employment.aspx
216. Indeed.com—http://www.indeed.jobs/
217. Insight Global Inc.—https://www.insightglobal.net/careers/careers-at-insight-global/
218. Instagram—https://www.instagram.com/about/jobs/
219. Intel—http://jobs.intel.com/
220. Audi—https://www.audiusa.com/about/careers
221. Intercontinental Hotels Group—http://careers.ihg.com/
222. Intuit Inc.—http://careers.intuit.com/
223. It Works!—http://www.myitworks.com/crazywrap/Wrapreneur/
224. J. M. Smucker—http://www.jmsmucker.com/smuckers-careers
225. Jack in the Box—http://careers.jackintheboxinc.com/
226. Jamba Juice—http://www.jambajuice.com/connect-with-jamba/careers
227. Janus—https://www.janus.com/careers
228. Jason's Deli—http://www.jasonsdeli.com/careers
229. JBS USA—http://jbssa.com/careers/opportunities/
230. Jeunesse Global—https://www.jeunesseglobal.com/en-US/financial-rewards
231. Jimmy John's—https://www.jimmyjohns.com/contact-us/jobs/
232. JM Family Enterprises Inc—http://m.jmfamily.com/careers.html
233. Jobs2Careers—http://www.jobs2careers.com/careers.php
234. Johnson & Johnson—http://www.careers.jnj.com/home
235. Juicy Couture—https://www.juicycouture.com/careers
236. Kaiser Permanente—http://www.kaiserpermanentejobs.org/default.aspx
237. Karl Lagerfeld—http://www.karl.com/experience/en/careers/
238. Kasper Group—http://kasper.com/index.php/careers/
239. KEEN—http://www.keenfootwear.com/jointeam.aspx
240. Kellogg Co.—http://www.kelloggcareers.com/global/home.html
241. Keurig—http://www.keuriggreenmountain.com/en/JobSeekers/Overview.aspx
242. KFC—https://jobs.kfc.com/

243. Kimberly-Clark—http://www.careersatkc.com/home.aspx
244. Kimley-Horn & Associates—http://www.kimley-horn.com/join-our-team
245. Kimpton Hotels and Resorts—https://www.kimptonhotels.com/careers
246. Kmart—http://www.kmart.com.au/jobs
247. Koch Industries—http://www.kochcareers.com/
248. Kohl's—http://kohlscareers.com/search-and-apply/
249. KPMG LLP—http://us-jobs.kpmg.com/
250. Krispy Kreme—https://www.krispykreme.com/careers/info
251. Kroger—https://jobs.kroger.com/
252. Krystal—http://krystal.com/careers/
253. L. L. Bean Inc.—https://llbeancareers.com/
254. L'Oreal—http://www.loreal.com/careers/home-careers
255. La Quinta Inns—http://lq.jobs/
256. Land O'Lakes Inc.—https://www.landolakesinc.com/Careers
257. LEK Consulting—http://www.lek.com/join-lek
258. Lending Club—https://www.lendingclub.com/public/careers.action
259. Lenovo—https://www.lenovocareers.com/
260. LG Corp.—http://www.lg.com/us/careers
261. Liberty Global—http://www.libertyglobal.com/careers/
262. Liberty Mutual—https://www.libertymutualgroup.com/careers
263. LinkedIn—https://www.linkedin.com/company-beta/1337/jobs
264. Little Caesars Pizza—https://littlecaesars.com/en-us/Join-Our-Brand/Careers
265. Logan's Roadhouse Grill—http://www.logansroadhouse.jobs/
266. Lole—http://www.lolewomen.com/careers/
267. Longhorn Steakhouse—http://www.longhornsteakhouse.com/careers
268. Longview International Technical—http://www.longview-inc.com/careers
269. Loyal Source Government—http://www.loyalsource.com/jobs/
270. LVMH Fragrance Brands—https://www.lvmh.com/talents/work-with-us/job-offers/

271. MAC—https://www.maccosmetics.com/employment
272. Maple Leaf Foods—http://www.mapleleaffoods.com/careers/
273. Marc Jacobs—https://www.marcjacobs.com/jobs
274. MarketSmith—http://www.marketsmithinc.com/we-are-marketsmith/join-our-team/
275. MarketSource Inc.—http://marketsource.jobs/
276. Marriott Brands—http://www.marriott.com/careers/default.mi?stop_mobi=yes
277. Mars Inc.—http://www.mars.com/global/careers
278. Mary Kay—http://www.marykay.com/en-US/About-Mary-Kay/EmploymentMaryKay
279. Mass Mutual—https://careers.massmutual.com/
280. Mavodo Group Inc.—http://careers.movadogroup.com/working-here/
281. MCA Corporation—https://mcappliance.com/careers
282. McCain Foods—http://www.mccainusa.com/Careers/
283. McDonald's—https://www.mcdonalds.com/us/en-us/careers.html
284. McKesson—https://careers.mckesson.com/
285. MeetMe—http://www.meetme.com/apps/careers
286. Meetup—http://www.meetup.com/jobs/
287. Meredith Corporation—http://www.meredith.com/careers
288. Meridian Health—https://www.meridianhealth.com/careers/
289. Met Life—https://www.metlife.com/careers/index.html
290. MGM Resorts International—http://www.mgmresortscareers.com/
291. Michael Kors—http://www.michaelkors.com/mobile/browse/common/staticContent.jsp?slotId=2800511
292. Microsoft—https://careers.microsoft.com/
293. Minute Key—https://www.minutekey.com/careers
294. Mio—http://www.mioglobal.com/en-us/careers.htm
295. Misfit Shine—https://misfit.com/jobs
296. Mohawk Industries Inc.—http://mohawkindustries.jobs/
297. Mondelez International—http://www.mondelezinternational.com/careers

298. Monster.com—https://careers.monster.com/
299. Morgan Stanley—http://www.morganstanley.com/people-opportunities/opportunities.html
300. Motorola—http://www.motorolacareers.com/
301. Mutual of Omaha—http://www.mutualofomaha.com/careers/
302. National Instruments—https://www.ni.com/careers/
303. NCR Corp.—http://www.ncr.com/careers
304. Nestle—http://www.nestle.com/jobs
305. NetApp—http://www.netapp.com/us/careers/
306. Newell Rubbermaid Inc.—http://careers.newellrubbermaid.com/
307. New Balance—https://jobs.newbalance.com/
308. News Corporation—http://newscorp.com/careers/
309. Next Step Living—http://www.nextstepliving.com/green-jobs
310. Nike—http://jobs.nike.com/
311. Nine West—http://careers.ninewest.com/
312. Nivea—http://www.niveausa.com/about-us/beiersdorf/Career
313. Nordstrom—http://about.nordstrom.com/careers/
314. North American Power—https://www.napower.com/careers
315. Novo Nordisk Inc.—http://www.novonordisk-us.com/careers.html
316. Nugget Markets—https://www.nuggetmarket.com/careers/
317. NuStar Energy—http://nustarenergy.com/en-us/careers/Pages/CareersMain.aspx
318. O'Charley's—http://ocharleys.jobs/
319. O. C. Tanner Co.—http://www.octanner.com/careers.html
320. Ocwen Financial Corp.—https://jobs.ocwen.com/
321. Office Depot—http://jobs.officedepot.com/
322. Olive Garden—http://www.olivegarden.com/careers
323. Omni Hotels & Resorts—https://www.omnihotels.com/careers
324. On the Border Mexican Grill & Cantina—https://www.ontheborder.com/employment
325. Opera Media Works—http://operamediaworks.com/careers
326. Orkin Pest Control—https://careers.orkin.com/

327. Outback Steakhouse—https://www.outback.com/careers
328. Panasonic—http://shop.panasonic.com/careers
329. Panda Express—https://www.pandacareers.com/find-career
330. Panera Bread—http://panerapeople.com/
331. Papa John's Pizza—http://www.papajohns.com/careers/
332. Parmalat—http://parmalat.co.za/page/careers
333. Patagonia—http://www.patagonia.com/careers
334. PCL Construction—http://www.pcl.com/careers/pages/Search-Careers.aspx
335. Peak Capital Partners—http://peakcapitalpartners.com/peak-capital-team/
336. PEG Bandwidth—http://www.pegbandwidth.com/jobs/
337. PepsiCo—http://www.pepsicojobs.com/
338. Perdue Farms—http://www.perduefarms.com/careers/
339. Perkins Coie LLP—https://www.perkinscoie.com/en/about-us/careers/laterals/job-listings/index.html
340. Perkins Restaurant and Bakery—http://www.perkinsrestaurants.com/careers/
341. P. F. Chang's China Bistro—http://jobs.pfchangs.com/
342. Phillips 66—http://phillips66.jobs/
343. PHunware—http://www.phunware.com/company/careers/
344. Pilgrim's Pride—http://www.pilgrims.com/contact-us/careers.aspx
345. Pinnacle Foods—http://stage.pinnaclefoods.com/Careers/Current+Opportunities
346. Pinterest—https://careers.pinterest.com/
347. Pizza Hut—https://jobs.pizzahut.com/
348. Plante & Moran PLLC—http://www.plantemoran.com/careers/pages/landing.aspx
349. Plexus Worldwide—http://www.plexus.com/careers/current-opportunities
350. Polo Ralph Lauren—http://global.ralphlauren.com/en-us/About/Pages/careers.aspx?
351. Popeye's Louisiana Kitchen—http://popeyes.jobs/

352. Prairie Farms Dairy—http://www.jobs.net/jobs/prairie-farms-dairy/en-us/
353. Prepay Nation—http://prepaynation.com/careers/
354. Prescient—http://www.prescient.com/careers/
355. Price Waterhouse Coopers—http://www.pwc.com/gx/en/careers.html
356. Primerica—http://www.primerica.com/public/opportunity.html
357. Principle Solutions Group—http://www.principlesolutions.com/content/careers
358. Proctor and Gamble—http://us.pgcareers.com/
359. Protiviti Inc.—http://www.protiviti.com/India-en/Pages/Apply-to-Protiviti.aspx
360. Prudential—http://jobs.prudential.com/
361. Publix—http://corporate.publix.com/careers
362. PulteGroup Inc.—http://pultegroupinc.com/careers/default.aspx
363. Puma—http://about.puma.com/en/careers/jobs-at-puma
364. PVH Corporation—http://www.pvh.com/people/work-with-us
365. Quest Nutrition—https://www.questnutrition.com/careers
366. Quick Trip—http://www.quiktrip.com/Jobs
367. Quicken Loans Inc.—http://www.quickenloanscareers.com/
368. Quiznos Subs—http://www.quiznos.com/About/Careers.aspx
369. Rail Careers—http://railcareers.net.au/
370. Ralph Lauren—http://global.ralphlauren.com/en-us/About/Pages/careers.aspx?
371. Randstad—https://www.randstadusa.com/jobs/careers-at-randstad/
372. Razer—http://careers.razerzone.com/
373. Red Lobster—https://www.redlobster.com/work-with-us
374. Red Robin Gourmet Burgers—http://redrobin.jobs/
375. Reebok—Adidas Group—https://careers.adidas-group.com/brands/reebok
376. Regal Wings—https://www.regalwings.com/btm/careers.html
377. REI Recreational Equipment—http://rei.jobs/
378. Response Team 1—http://www.responseteam1.com/careers/

379. RetailMeNot—https://www.retailmenot.com/corp/careers/
380. Rich Products Corp.—https://careers.rich.com/
381. Riot Games—http://www.riotgames.com/careers
382. Riverbed—http://www.riverbed.com/about/careers/
383. Road Runner Sports—http://www.roadrunnersportsjobs.com/
384. Robert W. Baird & Co.—http://bairdcareers.com/
385. Roche Group—http://www.roche.com/careers.htm
386. Romano's Macaroni Grill—http://www.macaronigrillcareers.com/
387. Ross—https://corp.rossstores.com/careers
388. Ruby Tuesday—http://careers.rubytuesday.com/
389. Ruth's Chris Steak House—http://www.ruthschris.com/careers/
390. Ryan—http://www.ryan.com/Careers?l=en-us
391. Sain Store—http://www.sainstore.com/careers
392. Salesforce.com—http://www.salesforce.com/company/careers/
393. Samsung—https://careers.us.samsung.com/careers/svc/app/viewSearchJob
394. Sanderson Farms—http://www.sandersonfarms.com/company/careers/
395. Sanyo—https://www.sanyodenki.co.jp/contents/careers/en/list_01.html
396. Saputo Inc.—http://www.saputo.com/futures-candidates/careers/default.aspx?langtype=4105
397. SAS Institute Inc.—http://www.sas.com/en_us/careers.html
398. Sbarro—http://www.sbarro.com/careers/
399. Sears—http://jobs.sears.com/
400. Seattle's Best Coffee—http://www.starbucks.com/careers
401. Sheetz—https://www.sheetz.com/jobopenings/job_openings.jsp
402. Skechers—http://www.skecherscareers.com/
403. Sky Zone—http://www.skyzone.com/timonium/About-Us/Jobs
404. Smithfield Foods—http://www.smithfieldfoods.com/careers
405. Snagajob.com—http://www.snagajob.com/about/careers/
406. Soliant Health—http://www.soliant.com/jobs/
407. Sonic Drive-In—https://www.sonicdrivein.com/jobs/corporate

408. Sony—http://www.sony.com/en_us/SCA/careers/overview.html
409. Southwest Airlines—https://www.southwest.com/html/about-southwest/careers/
410. Spherion Staffing—http://www.spherion.com/job-seekers/
411. Sprint—http://careers.sprint.com/
412. St. John—http://www.sjkcareers.com/
413. Staples—http://careers.staples.com/
414. Starbucks—http://www.starbucks.com/careers
415. Starwood Hotels & Resorts—http://www.starwoodhotels.com/corporate/candidate.html
416. State Farm Inc.—https://www.statefarm.com/careers
417. State Street Corporation—http://www.statestreet.com/about/careers.html
418. Steak 'n Shake—http://www.steaknshake.com/careers
419. Steven Madden—http://www.stevemadden.com/content.jsp?pageName=Careers
420. Stryker Corporation—http://careers.stryker.com/
421. Subway—http://www.subway.com/en-us/careers
422. Sweet Frog Premium—http://sweetfrog.com/employment-opportunities
423. Taco Bell—http://jobs.tacobell.com/index.html
424. Taco Mac—http://tacomac.com/careers/
425. Tahari—http://www.stylecareers.com/candidates/joblist.asp?JALLPOSTS=Elie-b-Tahari
426. TEK Systems Inc.—https://www.teksystems.com/en/it-careers
427. Texas Instruments—http://careers.ti.com/search-jobs/
428. Texas Roadhouse—https://www.texasroadhouse.com/careers
429. TGI Fridays—https://www.tgifridays.com/careers/
430. The Cheat Sheet—http://www.cheatsheet.com/jobs/
431. The Clymb—http://www.theclymb.com/careers.aspx
432. The Container Store—http://www.containerstore.com/careers/index.html
433. The Hartford—https://www.thehartford.com/careers

434. The HCI Group—https://www.thehcigroup.com/healthcare-it-careers
435. The North Face—https://www.thenorthface.com/about-us/careers.html
436. Tim Horton Careers—http://www.timhortons.com/us/en/corporate/restaurant-opportunities.php
437. Timberland—https://www.timberland.com/about-us/careers.html
438. Time Inc.—http://www.timeinc.com/careers/
439. Title Boxing Club—http://titleboxingclub.com/careers/
440. TJX Holdings (TJ Maxx, Marshall's)—https://www.tjx.com/career/careers_opportunities.html
441. TNH Advanced Specialty Pharmacy—https://tnhpharmacy.com/careers/
442. T-mobile—https://tmobile.jobs/
443. Tommy Hilfiger—https://global.tommy.com/int/en/careers/work-at-tommy/17
444. Toshiba—http://www.toshiba.com/tic/inside-toshiba/careers
445. Total System Services Inc.—http://tsys.com/careers/
446. Totes—https://www.totes.com/careers
447. Tough Mudder—https://toughmudder.com/careers
448. Toyota—http://www.toyota.com/usa/careers/
449. Tumblr—https://www.tumblr.com/jobs
450. Twilio—https://www.twilio.com/company/jobs
451. Twitter, Inc.—https://careers.twitter.com/en.html
452. Tyson Foods—http://www.tysonfoodscareers.com/Hillshire-Brands.aspx
453. UBS—https://www.ubs.com/global/en/about_ubs/careers.html
454. Ultimate Software—http://www.ultimatesoftware.com/careers-at-ultimate
455. Under Armour—http://www.underarmour.jobs/talent-areas/corporate/
456. Unilever North America—https://www.unileverusa.com/careers/
457. United Airlines—https://www.united.com/web/en-US/content/company/career/default.aspx

458. United Health Group—https://careers.unitedhealthgroup.com/landing-pages/tricare
459. Universal Studios—http://www.universalorlandojobs.com/
460. Unum—http://www.unumgroup.com/Careers/CareerOpportunities.aspx
461. USAA—https://search.usaajobs.com/us/en-us/search-jobs/XsjgP
462. Vacasa—https://www.vacasa.com/careers/
463. Vaco—http://www.vaco.com/for-candidates.html
464. Valero Energy—https://valero.taleo.net/careersection/2/jobsearch.ftl?lang=en
465. Versace—http://careers.versace.com/en
466. VF—http://www.vfc.com/careers
467. Viacom—http://www.viacomcareers.com/
468. VIA Rail—https://career.viarail.ca/en/home
469. Vine—https://vine.co/jobs
470. Visionaire Partners—http://www.visionairepartners.com/looking-forajob.html
471. VK Knowlton—http://www.vkk.com/careers/
472. VM Ware Inc.—https://careers.vmware.com/
473. VRX—https://www.myvrx.com/careers/
474. W. L. Gore and Associates—https://www.gore.com/careers
475. Waffle House—http://www.wafflehouse.com/whcareers/
476. Walmart—http://careers.walmart.com/
477. Walt Disney World—http://wdw.disneycareers.com/en/default/
478. Wawa—https://www.wawa.com/CorporateOpportunities.aspx
479. Wegman's Food Markets—www.wegmans.com/careers
480. Wellcare Health—https://www.wellcare.com/Corporate/Careers
481. Wellpoint—http://careers.antheminc.com/
482. Wells Fargo—https://www.wellsfargo.com/about/careers/
483. WellStar Health System—http://wellstar.jobs/
484. Wendy's—https://careers.wendys.com/
485. Western Union—http://corporate.westernunion.com/careers/index.html

486. WestRock—https://www.westrock.com/en/careers
487. Whataburger—http://whataburger.com/careers
488. Whirlpool—http://www.whirlpoolcareers.com/
489. White Castle—http://careers.whitecastle.com/
490. White Wave Foods—http://www.whitewave.com/careers
491. Whole Foods Markets—http://www.wholefoodsmarket.com/careers
492. Wolverine Worldwide—http://www.wolverineworldwide.com/careers/
493. Workday Inc.—http://www.workday.com/company/careers.php
494. World Wide Tech Inc.—https://www2.wwt.com/careers/
495. Wyndham Worldwide—http://careers.wyndhamworldwide.com/jobs
496. Xpanxion—http://www.xpanxion.com/careers.html
497. Zappos—http://jobs.jobvite.com/zappos
498. Zaxby's—https://www.zaxbys.com/join-the-team/
499. Zenith Insurance—http://www.zenithinsurance.com.ng/careers.aspx
500. Zoo Atlanta—http://www.zooatlanta.org/home/careers

Use the FREE space below to freestyle!
Grab some colored pencils and doodle, draw, brainstorm, reflect or whatever!

Leslie's Listening!

OK...let's talk! I wanted this book to be interactive. I would love to partner with you as you become inspired, empowered, and informed. Here are a few questions for you to consider as you ponder what you want from this chapter.

What job do you have presently?

_____
_____

Is it the career field of your choice?

_____
_____

If so, how would you like to advance from where you are?

_____
_____

If at present you are not in a field of your choice, what is your career interest?

_____
_____

How are you going to start working on the career of your choice today?

_____
_____

Is there anything that I have not asked that you would like to share?

_____
_____
_____
_____
_____

OK! Let's get to WORK!

Two

FREE Stuff

Greetings, Beautiful Friends! ☺

Let me just preface this section by screaming, "I love FREE STUFF!" Whenever I get free certificates via e-mail or "snail mail," it's like they burn a hole in my pocket. I have to spend them right away! Whether they're "just-because" gifts or loyalty customer perks, I'm on it! They can be from Chick-fil-A, Smoothie King, Things Remembered, Sears, Kohl's, Starbucks, Staples, Shutterfly, Wendy's, Chili's, TGI Fridays, or wherever! Those gifts never reach an expiration date!

You may see free coupons that come in the mail. But are you aware of all the loads and loads of free stuff that is offered just to get you to try a new product or reintroduce you to an old one?

Check out links in this chapter to some amazing freebies that you've probably never heard of. One of my favorite freebie sites is Freebie-Depot. com. I have called on Tim Pearsall several times to serve as an expert in my articles. He is introducing this chapter, and I've got the link to his website! Now, that is really a special treat! You will love it! At the end of the chapter, feel free to answer questions that might help you get freebies you desire.

Thanks so much for your support, and have a great week! Happy Reading and Research!

Sincerely,

Leslie

Can you tell me about FREE stuff?

"Information about free stuff is important to me because it makes me aware of brand recognition, products, services, retailers, restaurants, etc. and allows me to try it before I buy it. This can prove valuable. It can get me on the list of a particular retailer/product. If I sample an edible product, I am more inclined to purchase the product (provided I like it) than I would have by just seeing the packaging. It allows me to share the information regarding the products/services with others. In regards to free stuff, as it relates to food, I would like to have the nutritional facts. I would like to know where the products can be purchased for future use. How can I get free samples?"

— *Anne Williams-Aplin is retired and loves shopping and freebies.*

**Perspective & Words of Advice
from *Leslie's Lane: The Book!*
FREE Stuff Expert**

"There are two great ways to maximize the number of freebies you receive. First, follow and monitor "free stuff" websites like Freebie Depot or Fat Wallet. They scour the web and find all the offers and essentially do the work for you. Second, sign up for sample box sites that work directly with multiple major manufacturers to get samples directly to consumers. PINCHme and Sample Source are great sites that send you boxes of samples (often with ten or more products) on a monthly basis. Most sites that list free offers also have daily e-mail newsletters. Since samples are often claimed quickly, these mailing lists will keep you abreast of offers as they become available—giving you the best shot at success. Sign up for your favorite brand, retailer or restaurant's e-mail list. Most companies market directly to consumers via e-mail offering free coupons, new product samples, recipes and other special discounts and promotions. Often these are exclusive offers that are only provided to e-mail subscribers. Ask. You would be surprised what you can get for free if you simply ask. Send an e-mail or letter asking for free samples and coupons. When you are at your favorite retailer, ask if they have any samples or freebies. They might just give you a product to try or even a promotional t-shirt!"

— *Tim Pearsall is Webmaster, Creator and CEO (Chief Everything Officer) of Freebie Depot.*

Leslie's Lessons—Five Tips at a Glance! Check Out Some of the Best FREE-Stuff Websites

1. http://www.freebie-depot.com/
2. http://www.latestfreestuff.co.uk/
3. www.freecycle.org
4. www.TotallyFreeStuff.com
5. www.thefreesite.com

Leslie's Litany—Three Books to Read! Check Out Some of the Best FREE-Stuff Books

1. *Gobs and Gobs of FREE Stuff!* by Matthew Lesko and Mary Ann Martello
2. *FREE: Comprehensive Directory for Getting Everything for FREE* by J. Charles
3. *How to Get FREE Stuff* by K. C. McAllister

Leslie's Lane The Book!
Expert Info at a Glance!
Company: Freebie Depot
Website: http://www.freebie-depot.com/
Facebook: https://www.facebook.com/Freebie-Depotcom-288121886910/?fref=ts
Twitter: @FreebieDepot
Instagram: @freebiedepot

My motto is, "why pay for anything that you can get for FREE?!" I love all things free! Imagine my excitement when I discovered FreebieDepot.com. I have interviewed Tim Pearsall for several *ESSENCE* articles. His site has a wealth of information! Get FREE samples, FREE birthday goodies, FREE groceries, FREE makeup, FREE calendars, and more! Please check out their link as well as several others:
http://www.freebie-depot.com/
http://www.latestfreestuff.co.uk/
www.freecycle.org
www.TotallyFreeStuff.com
www.thefreesite.com
www.getitfree.us

Let's add one more book to your reading list! *How to Shop for FREE: Shopping Secrets for Smart Women Who Love to Get Something for Nothing* is by Kathy Spencer and Samantha Rose.

Ready to get fit? Why not do it for FREE? It's important to me to work out several days a week. You can find full-length workout videos at https://www.fitnessblender.com/videos. Be sure to keep your ear to the ground for fitness trainers and centers offering FREE workout sessions.

Free Friday Downloads from Kroger are a hit for me. Make sure you have a loyalty card and sign up online. It'll come in your inbox every week.

Oh heavens! I absolutely LOVE Shutterfly!!! They have great products! You can personalize anything from cups, mugs, and tote bags to calendars, stationery, and home décor. They offer FREE gifts and products on a regular basis. I take advantage of it all the time. I am always pleased with how everything about them looks! Like their Facebook page and sign up with them at www.shutterfly.com to get freebies and discounts often.

Ready to get to know more about your credit score? Knowing your scores is really important. It impacts much of what we can get or purchase such as a job, car, home, utilities, and phone and cable services. Order your FREE credit reports from Experian, Transunion, and Equifax!

https://www.creditkarma.com/
https://www.freecreditreport.com/
https://www.freescoreonline.com/
http://www.myfico.com/
https://www.annualcreditreport.com/
www.experian.com
www.transunion.com
www.equifax.com

You can get FREE help with finances with the Live Richer Challenge! I became acquainted with Tiffany "The Budgetnista" Aliche when I wrote a *Black Enterprise* magazine article. She is so amazing; I asked her to introduce the chapter on discounts. I am particularly impressed by her Live Richer Challenge. This online financial challenge has empowered more than sixty-five thousand women from all fifty states and eighty countries. Check out this site: www.livericherchallenge.com. She is the author of *The One Week Budget* and *Live Richer Challenge*. Each of her social media sites boasts thousands of followers!

Get FREE remote help with your computer and more with TeamViewer! I love this! Thanks to my beautiful sister Sylathia Johnson for telling me about this! I don't know a whole lot about computers! OK. I'm not at all computer-savvy. In the past, when something went wrong, my sister "Sissie" would walk me through it on the phone. Now, that's a thing of the past with awesome technology. She now logs in remotely with the program and fixes my computer! How cool is that! Please click on this link: www.teamviewer.com

Create your own radio show or television show for FREE! Always wanted your own radio show or television show? Want to do a podcast? I certainly have and do! I would love to have a Leslie's Lane radio show and Leslie's Lane television show! Until I get my big break, I'll create my own radio show on BlogTalk and television show on YouTube! Why don't you join me? Well…you too can do it for FREE! Give it a try!

http://www.blogtalkradio.com/

https://www.entrepreneur.com/article/229284

Ready to plan your family reunion? There's nothing like spending time with your beautiful family. My family reunion began in 1978. Since then, every two years, the Dukes-Murphy-Burgess Family Reunion takes place. We are always looking for special resources, information, and freebies during our planning. A great resource is this FREE Family Reunion Workshop! Link: http://visitatlantasdekalbcounty.com/reunions/. Check in with the Convention and Visitors Bureau (CVB) for freebies in the city in which you plan to visit for your family reunion.

UNCLAIMED MONEY! FREE MONEY!!!!

Are you aware that billions of dollars owed to Americans go unclaimed each year? You or one of your loved ones can be included! Check out my *Black Enterprise* article on unclaimed cash! Just click this link: http://www.blackenterprise.com/mag/free-money/. Also, check out these links:

http://www.missingmoney.com/

https://www.usa.gov/unclaimed-money

https://www.unclaimed.org/

https://entp.hud.gov/dsrs/refunds/

http://www.missingmoney.com/

I think this is a wonderful program. The US Department of Agriculture presents a Summer Food Service Program (SFSP) annually. The free meals are for children up to age eighteen. For more information, Call 1-866-3-HUNGRY or go to http://www.whyhunger.org/findfood. More information is available at http://www.fns.usda.gov/sfsp/summer-food-service-program.

Gone are the days that you have to spend loads of money on invitations and stamps for your special events. You can now create beautiful "e-vites" to your friends for FREE! So go ahead! Plan your parties, bridal showers, baby showers, and more with these FREE special-events sites:

www.eventbrite.com

www.events.org

www.yelp.com

www.eventful.com

www.myevent.com

www.lanyrd.com

www.facebook.com

Don't miss The Free and Cheap List from my hero, Clark Howard. Check out info on FREE conference calls, directory assistance, online college classes, teacher software, books, music, tax filings, household products, and more! Please check out loads of discounts, products, services, and resources at http://www.clarkhoward.com/the-free-and-cheap-list!

Take advantage of the Free Phone Program with SafeLink Wireless – Go to this site to see if you qualify - https://www.safelinkwireless.com.

Use the FREE space below to freestyle!
Grab some colored pencils and doodle, draw, brainstorm, reflect or whatever!

Leslie's Listening!
OK…let's talk! I wanted this book to be interactive. I would love to partner with you as you become inspired, empowered, and informed. Here are a few questions for you to consider as you ponder what you want from this chapter.

What types of items would you like to get for FREE?

_____

_____

Are you willing to serve on panels or do surveys to get freebies? Which ones are of interest to you?

_____

_____

How do you feel about going to freebie sites and registering to receive e-mails?

_____

_____

Is there anything that I have not asked that you would like to share?

_____

_____

_____

_____

_____

OK! Let's get to WORK!

Three

FREE and Discount Travel

Greetings, Beautiful Friends! 😊

As I shared in the previous chapter, I love all things FREE! Plus, I love traveling! And when you mix the two, that's one exciting cocktail of fun! I married young and decided that when my children became adults, I would travel all over the place. But you know what? I have found that you can travel or take a vacation whenever you like on even the most modest budget.

For individuals, couples, immediate families, and family reunions who would like to travel, check out these links featuring all types of awesome ways to vacay! You will find information on discount hotels, cruises, plane tickets, and more. And when you reach your destination, you can actually find FREE attractions depending upon where you are residing in the city. As a special treat, I have included several Leslie's Leisure articles in this chapter.

Calling all fellow travel writers! You probably already know that you can take press trips! I love this part of our job! As long as you agree to write an article for your particular publication or blog, you can gain entrance into the wonderful world of special perks! Please keep in mind that the host organization can be very strict and may require a large circulation or following on Twitter and Instagram.

Please check information in this chapter on how to sign up for press trips. Also, you will find listings of CVBs throughout the world. At the end of this chapter, you will find questions to answer to help you best budget for your next trip. Thanks so much for your support, and have a great week! Happy Reading and Research!

Sincerely,

Leslie

Can you tell me about FREE and discount travel?

"Having information on free and discount travel is very important to me because it provides financial savings. Any money saved affords me an opportunity to enjoy other things such as shopping and/or purchasing souvenirs for friends and family. As a savvy shopper who compares and searches for the best bargains, I am always seeking reduced, discounted and free items. Besides, why pay full price for anything? I, like most people, usually don't have the extra money for elaborate travel. Therefore, any and all discounts are welcomed. What are the many ways in which I can acquire free and/or discount travel without committing to a time-share presentation or joining a travel club?"
— *Neva J. Jones, a senior analyst for a national airline, loves to travel and explore the world both here and abroad.*

**Perspective & Words of Advice
from *Leslie's Lane: The Book!*
Travel Expert**

"*Travel!* We all want to visit faraway places, explore various cultures and people, enjoy great food and experience once-in-a-lifetime moments. When adventure calls, it can be very expensive. But there are ways to travel the world for free or at a discount. *Volunteer.* Farming, teaching, building schools and working to make changes in depressed communities is one way. *Couch surf.* This is appealing to those who like meeting people and making new friends around the world. Couching surfing is just as it sounds. You have a chance to stay in the home of a local host for a few nights. *House-sit.* You'll have the whole house to yourself while the owners are out of town. Keep the plants and pets happy while you have a chance to explore a new city. Go to the local tourism office and ask for any free tickets or discounted entry fees. Visit museums and attractions on free days."

— *Annita Stokes Thomas is a travel journalist and the host of* Travel Bags with Annita Radio Show.

Leslie's Lessons—Five Tips at a Glance! Check Out Some of the Best FREE Travel Websites

1. Free Entrance Days at National Parks—https://www.nps.gov/plany-ourvisit/fee-free-parks.htm
2. 101 FREE Things to Do in London—http://www.visitlondon.com/things-to-do/budget-london/101-free-things-to-do-in-london#1gfuTh4iHr1CAEpm.97
3. 101 FREE Things to Do in Chicago—http://www.timeout.com/chicago/things-to-do/101-things-to-do-in-chicago
4. FREE Things to Do in New York City—http://www.nycgo.com/free
5. FREE Things to do in Orlando—http://www.visitorlando.com/things-to-do/free-things-to-do/

Leslie's Litany—Three Books to Read! Check Out Some of the Best Discount Travel Books

1. *Fly for FREE* by Bryan Adams
2. *101 Money-Saving Travel Tips* by Daniel Davidson
3. *The Penny Pincher's Guide to Luxury Travel* by Joel L. Widzer

Leslie's Lane The Book!
Expert Info at a Glance!
Company: Travel Bags with Annita
Website: http://www.travelbagswithannita.com/
Facebook: https://www.facebook.com/travelbagswithannita/?fref=ts
Twitter: @AnnitaNFriends
Instagram: @annitanfriends

As many of you know, I like all things FREE and nearly FREE! Vacations and travel are no exception. As you plan your activities and attractions to visit, I wanted to share a few tips and a little info to help you save money!

One of the first things I typically do is contact the Convention and Visitors Bureau of the city I would like to visit. They are always eager to help. Ask for the names and contact information of sites and attractions that are free and open to the public. Check out this link to convention and visitors bureaus: http://www.cvent.com/rfp/us-cvb-directory-84666a30191e407e-a182af64c488696a.aspx.

Next, if there are local newspapers in your area, request information on travel articles that cover free attractions in various cities, states, or countries. A fun thing to do is take your children to the neighborhood library in search of specific books and research periodicals on free places to go while on vacation. Ask to check out the digital book entitled *101 FREE Things to Do in Europe* by Gabe Lara.

You certainly want to consider getting a CityPass if the city you are visiting offers it. I enjoyed the use of one when Tony and I visited Philadelphia for July 4 and New York City for the Christmas holidays last year. Additional cities are Atlanta, Boston, Chicago, Dallas, and Houston. You get prepaid, bundled admission to the city's top attractions at up to 50 percent off the regular price. Check it out at www.citypass.com.

Travel clubs are great sources for information. Because these individuals have traveled throughout the United States and the world, they can be helpful. You may also consider joining an organization of this nature if it will save you money in the long run.

I really love zoos! So whenever I travel with my family, I make sure to visit the zoo in that particular city. While some zoos charge a fee, the exceptional St. Louis Zoo is FREE! Special thanks to my friend Dorothea Williams and sorority sister Carolyn Kidd Royal (we're married to brothers) for giving me this tip on the St. Louis Zoo! They inspired this section of the book on FREE zoos. Check out this link: http://www.trekaroo.com/list/free-zoos-across-the-us.

"Marry Me (or Make Me)—Fly FREE!"

It's always cool to work with an airline! My daughter Antasha is a flight attendant, and my husband Tony and I fly for FREE! In fact, most airlines allow parents and children to fly for FREE. You get a companion pass for your spouse or other special individual. Plus, you get Buddy Passes. If you want to travel the world at no cost, consider working for an airline! Please click on this link for the list of the largest airlines in North America: http://en.wikipedia. org/wiki/List_of_largest_airlines_in_North_America. You can then Google the name of the airline and careers. I've provided five here.

1. Delta—http://www.deltajobs.net/career_destinations.htm
2. American—http://careers.aa.com/en/ac/home
3. Southwest—https://www.southwest.com/html/about-southwest/ careers/index.html?clk=GFOOTER-ABOUT-CAREERS
4. United—http://www.united.com/web/en-US/content/company/ career/default.aspx
5. Air Canada—http://www.aircanada.com/en/about/career/index.html

When Antasha first became a flight attendant, she surprised me and took me to Buenos Aires, Argentina, in 2014! We've traveled a good deal since then. Recently, we went to Santiago, Chile. I especially like our overnight international trips. We have a strategy for traveling first class internationally for pennies on the dollar. On a trip that would have cost $4,000 to $6,000 each (for business class), we spent a little under $500 total (that's $250 each).

1. The night before, Antasha combs Delta's website for flights to nice destinations that have first-class sections that are practically empty. This assures us a seat in first class!
2. We use the plane as our hotel—we board late in the evening and fly all night. In first class, the seats convert into beds. Passengers get premium meals, great snacks, complimentary specialty beverages, hot towels, great headsets, and so much more! On the "plane hotel," you don't pay anything to spend the night!!!

3. We go on TripAdvisor or Expedia to find a four-star boutique or chained-brand hotel for one hundred dollars max nightly. We make sure it includes FREE breakfast and Wi-Fi. On the morning of our arrival, we go to the hotel, and they store the luggage while we tour all day.
4. We come back and check into the hotel and enjoy the beautiful room, lodging, and amenities such as receptions and so on.
5. The following morning, we check out, have them store our luggage, and spend the rest of the day touring until it's time to go to the airport. We then take the "plane hotel" home!

I love AARP! I was so excited when my husband hit the "Big 50" and we could join this exclusive club! They have such awesome deals and really give us great tips on saving money! So all you sassy seniors, check out this link: http://travel.aarp.org.

Are you interested in free things to do in cities not mentioned in the Top Ten? Just Google free things to do in _____, filling in the blank. For example when you search free things to do in Pensacola, Florida, at http://www.visit-pensacola.com/articles/affordable-vacations, one link you will find is 25 Fun FREE Things to Do in Pensacola.

If you're like me, you love searching great travel search engines for enormous discounts. I usually start out with TripAdvisor. It will search many sites simultaneously and uniquely for you. Plus, you can read excellent reviews from people vacationing just like you and me! Search luxury hotels first. You will be surprised at prices comparable to modest hotels. I also like Expedia because you can save by bundling hotels, flights, and car rentals. If you want to get great prices on flights—even at the last minute, go to Google flights. Check out these sites:

www.tripadvisor.com
www.kayak.com

www.expedia.com
www.hotels.com
www.priceline.com
www.hotwire.com
www.cheaptickets.com
www.googleflights.com
www.hipmunk.com
www.hotels.com
www.orbitz.com
www.travelocity.com

Well…not everyone likes to fly. My dear Aunt Helen often jokes, "Jesus said, 'Lo, I am with you.' So I'm not flying high in a plane." If, like my auntie, you prefer to stay on the ground, here are a few links to Amtrak for your train rides and Greyhound if you prefer to travel by bus. While we are speaking of buses, the Megabus is really cool! You can get tickets for as low as one dollar! How cool is that? My hero, Clark Howard, has given us the secret to the one-dollar tickets!

Megabus Discount tickets as low as one dollar:
http://www.megabus.com/
http://www.clark.com/secret-scoring-1-seats-megabus
Discount Tickets from Amtrak:
https://www.amtrak.com/deals
Discount Tickets from Greyhound:
https://www.greyhound.com/en/help-and-info/ticket-info/discounts

I love this! Groupon Getaways! Well, I love Groupon! It was the first discount savings site I was ever introduced to. In recent years, it has evolved and added travel to its immense savings platform. Please click on this link to purchase great discount vacations: https://www.groupon.com/getaways

All-inclusive vacations are simply awesome. They are exactly what the name implies. Your hotel room, meals, and drinks are included in your quoted price.

I remember when Tony and I took our first all-inclusive vacation to Aruba! We drank nonalcoholic strawberry daiquiris all day! Check out some of these links for vacation packages:
http://www.cheapcaribbean.com/deals/all-inclusive-vacation-packages.html
http://bookit.com/travel-ideas/all-inclusive/
http://www.sandals.com/all-inclusive-resorts/
https://www.jetblue.com/vacations/all-inclusive/
http://www.applevacations.com/all-inclusive/
http://www.vacationexpress.com/all-inclusive/
https://www.expedia.com/All-Inclusive-Vacations

**Use the FREE space below to freestyle!
Grab some colored pencils and doodle, draw, brainstorm,
reflect or whatever!**

An Exclusive Quote for *Leslie's Lane The Book!*
I asked my friend Brenda to share why all-inclusive vacations make for a really good idea.

> *The creation of the all-inclusive vacation packages revolutionized travel. Travelers are now able to enjoy their dream vacation without having to go into their pockets while travelling. Guests are able to pay for air, hotel, transfers, and many activities in full before travel has even begun. With some resorts, tipping is also already included in the packages. Guests are able to spread payments out over an eleven-month period, thus enabling them to plan some amazing getaways without breaking their budgets. Now many properties give guests resort credits to use during their stay. These credits can be used for spa treatments, excursions, weddings, tours, and so on. This has even greater enhanced the all-inclusive vacation.*
>
> *—**Brenda Washington-O'Neale**, Romance Travel Specialist with* With This Ring Destination Wedding and Honeymoon Travel Agency

Tony and I love taking cruises. We have taken our moms and their guests on several Carnival Cruises. We have gone with family. We have gone with friends. We were hooked when we took our first cruise in 1989 aboard the Norwegian Cruise Lines! We particularly loved our last cruise during the Chick-fil-A Operator Seminar. We were on Royal Caribbean Cruises and ended up getting a junior suite. I usually like to start by searching Expedia.com for cruises and go from there. You can Google best cruise deals to see articles, cruise line websites, and search engine sites.

One of my favorite things to do is simply to search the Internet to find free things to do! Enter "101 Free Things" and the state or country of your choice into a search engine. This will yield numerous links. I've already completed the following:

1. Free Entrance Days at National Parks—https://www.nps.gov/planyourvisit/fee-free-parks.htm

2. 101 FREE Things to Do in London—http://www.visitlondon. com/things-to-do/budget-london/101-free-things-to-do-in-london#1gfuTh4iHr1CAEpm.97
3. 101 FREE Things to Do in Chicago—http://www.timeout.com/ chicago/things-to-do/101-things-to-do-in-chicago
4. 101 FREE Things to Do in the South—http://www.southernliving. com/travel/101-free-things-to-do-in-the-south
5. 101 FREE Things to Do with Kids in Michigan—http://grkids. com/101-free-things-to-do-with-kids-in-michigan/
6. 101 FREE and Almost Free Things to Do in DC—https://washington.org/100-free-and-almost-free-things-do-dc
7. FREE Things to Do in New York City—http://www.nycgo.com/free
8. 100 FREE Things to Do in LA—http://www.discoverlosangeles.com/ blog/100-free-things-do-los-angeles-free-activities
9. FREE Attractions in Las Vegas—https://www.vegas.com/attractions/ free-attractions-las-vegas/
10. FREE Things to Do in Orlando—http://www.visitorlando.com/ things-to-do/free-things-to-do/

I, like so many others, have a bucket list. I steadily check it off every chance I get. One of those things on my bucket list is camping. I've never done so before. For all of you campers—whether first timers or many timers—check out Passport America Discount Camping Club. This club offers 50 percent off camping. Please click on this link: http://www.passportamerica.com/

Another great way to save on vacations is to research resort groups having multiple locations. One example is Vacation Myrtle Beach. They have great specials. They have fourteen beachfront properties that are quite budget friendly. We—myself, Antasha, and my goddaughter and niece Le Tonya—stayed at the Beach Cove Resort. We had a fabulous time and loved all the great amenities, which included beachfront condos, a lazy river, several pools, an arcade, free parking, a delicious restaurant, nearby golfing, kiddie activities, and so much more. Check it out at www.vacation-myrtlebeach.com.

I had an opportunity to meet Annita Stokes Thomas on a press trip a few years back. I found her to be a wealth of information. We really connected, and she invited me on her excellent radio show called *Travel Bags with Annita*. I discussed great discounts and savings. Her radio show provides awesome info on trips in the United States and abroad, vacation tips, and travel news. Please check out her website and blog! You'll be glad you did! She was nice enough to share this link to her article for this book: http://www.travelbagswithannita. com/5-tips-to-avoid-vacation-budget-busters/. It focuses on budgeting when you take your vacation.

Below, please find her expanded response to questions for this book on free and discount travel. I'm happy to see that a few of her answers correspond to my suggestions.

An Exclusive Article for *Leslie's Lane The Book!*
"Seven Ways to Travel for FREE or Discount" By Annita Stokes Thomas

1. Volunteer. When you think of volunteering when traveling, missionary work come to mind. While that's still an extraordinary way to help others while you also learn and grow, there are other ways to volunteer: farming, teaching, building schools, or working to make changes in depressed communities. You can take cruises, travel to destinations for short- or long-term projects, or take a road trip as part of your volunteer trip. Travel can be a great way to make an impact while helping others and seeing the world.

2. Work for an airline and fly free. Buckle up, adventure calls. Airlines are frequently hiring, and the competition can be fierce, but if you can score one of the coveted positions, you can fly to exotic destinations while working and explore countries around the world, using your flight benefits to fly free. And, the great majority of airlines allow you to bring along parents, siblings, and friends.

3. Couch surfing is appealing to those who like meeting people and making new friends around the world. Couch surfing is just as it sounds. You have a chance to stay in the home of a local host for a few

nights. Check out the website www.couchsurfing.com, where you will find like-minded hosts ready for you to come over for a stay. You will experience culture during meals, outings, and conversations.

4. If couch surfing feels a little too cozy, house sitting is another option. You'll have the whole house to yourself while the owners are out of town. Keep the plants and pets happy while you have a chance to explore a new city.

5. When visiting your favorite city, there's no need to join an expensive hosted tour. Stop by the local tourism office, grab a map and their local magazine featuring all the popular sites, and create your own walking tour with your personalized guide. While at the tourism office, ask for any free tickets or discounted entry fees.

6. Visit museums and attractions on free days. Check the local city's guide book where a list of attractions will share hours, directions, and free days.

7. Throughout the year while you're planning and daydreaming about your next vacation, use a credit card with benefits to pay as many of your expenses as possible. You will accumulate points which can be used for flights, hotels, cruises, and attractions. The more the merrier.

Use this space to list free and discount opportunities for you to vacay!!!

_____
_____
_____
_____
_____
_____
_____
_____
_____
_____

If you are a travel journalist such as myself, a travel blogger, or a radio or television travel-show host like Annita, please check out my chapter "Pursue Your Passion! Creating the Job of Your Dreams!" It shares details on how to take FREE press trips! Press trips for travel journalists are typically all-inclusive and include FREE airline tickets, hotels, meals, transportation, and more. You just have to be on assignment and agree to write an article.

My hubby and I were raised in Savannah, Georgia. It is a beautiful, historic city. If you want to tour the attractions and landmarks, start by going to this site: http://freesavannahtours.com/. Additionally, when you plan vacations to various cities and countries, remember to ask about free tours.

Use the FREE space below to freestyle!
Grab some colored pencils and doodle, draw, brainstorm, reflect or whatever!

I really like writing travel pieces for my Leslie's Lane blog. Enjoy a few excerpts from them.

Leslie's Leisure: Great Promotion Allows Discovery of Stunning Natural Beauty and Beaches of US Virgin Islands

https://leslieslane.wordpress.com/ 2016/05/21/leslies-leisure-great-promotion-allows-discovery-of-stunning-natural-beauty-and-beaches-of-u-s-virgin-islands/

Posted on May 21, 2016, by Leslie's Lane—
By Leslie E. Royal

As you plan your vacation this summer and fall, consider the the US Virgin Islands (USVI). The collective islands of St. Croix, St. Thomas, and St. John are beautiful locales allowing for a wonderful time of relaxation, fun tours, relishing their stunning natural beauty and taking leisurely strolls along the beach. These islands are an ideal locale for vacationing year round. If you are a United States citizen and don't have a passport, no worries. You don't need one! Click on this link and you are well on your way to a magnificent vacation with great discounts: http://www.visitusvi.com/package_and_promotions. Consider staying at one of these luxurious, upscale hotels and resorts.

St. Croix—The Buccaneer Hotel, Club Comanche Hotel St. Croix, Club St. Croix Beach Resort and Tennis Club, Divi Carina Bay Beach Resort & Casino, Holger Danske Hotel; Hotel Caravelle, Hotel on the Cay, Renaissance Carambola Beach Resort & Spa, Sand Castle on the Beach, Tamarind Reef Resort, Spa & Marina, and The Palms at Pelican Cove.

St. John—Caribbean Villas, Concordia Eco-Resort, Gallows Point Resort, Island Getaways, SIRENUSA Residences, and The Westin St. John Resort & Villas.

St. Thomas—Bolongo Bay Beach Resort, Emerald Beach Resort, Frenchman's Reef & Morning Star Marriott Resort, Galleon House Bed and Breakfast, Lindbergh Bay Hotel and Villas, Mafolie Hotel, Pavilions & Pools Villa Hotel, Sapphire Beach Condominium Resort, Sugar Bay Resort & Spa, The Green Iguana Hotel, and Windward Passage Hotel.

To learn more about the US Virgin Islands, you can visit their website: www.VisitUSVI.com.

Follow them on Twitter @USVITourism and Like them on Facebook at www.facebook.com/VisitUSVI to keep up with their future promotions, activities, and events.

Leslie's Leisure: Treat Yourself to a Valentine's Day Private Getaway! Escape to Sapelo Island Birdhouses

Posted on February 7, 2016, by Leslie's Lane
https://leslieslane.wordpress.com/2016/02/07/leslies-leisure-treat-yourself-to-a-valentines-day-private-getaway-at-the-sapelo-island-bird houses/

I began the New Year relaxed, refreshed, revived, and reinvigorated! I have my brief retreat on Sapelo Island to thank for that! Last year, my daughter Antasha and I were invited by the Sapelo Island Birdhouses to attend a Girls ONLY Weekend and Press Tour of this beautiful island located an hour outside of my hometown of Savannah, Georgia. We had a wonderful time! Please check out this link to find out a little more about the historic, picturesque island:
https://en.wikipedia.org/wiki/Sapelo_Island.

 If you would like to get away to a peaceful, serene place to commune with nature and enjoy quality time with your loved ones, you should certainly consider Sapelo Island. Accessible by plane or boat only, you will relish in the delightful ferry ride from the mainland as the gentle wind blows through your hair. Once on the island, you can enjoy:

- Spending your honeymoon in a romantic, secluded location
- Having an entertaining girls-only (in my case) or guys-only weekend
- Reconnecting and recoupling with your significant other
- Spending quality time with your family by relaxing on the beach, having a cookout
- Taking a one-person-only retreat to relax, reflect, and get inspired

The fabulous accommodations of each of the Sapelo Island Birdhouses…

Once you've decided to escape to this quiet, tranquil island, you want to take a look at the lodging. Sapelo Island Birdhouses offers great amenities in its exquisite cottages. Each cottage features an expressly designed theme, pillow-top queen beds, Wi-Fi, NetFlix-accessible flat-screen TVs with DVD players, golf cart rentals, beach towels, chairs and umbrellas, screened-in porch, high-thread-count line and plush bath towels and much more! Each has a gourmet kitchen with state-of-the-art appliances. Since there are no restaurants on the island, guests bring all their food. Check out their quite informative website, which provides more details: http://www.sapeloislandbirdhouses.com/.

Leslie's Leisure Presents Luxury Locales, Etcetera in Historic Savannah, Georgia

I've written two articles on Savannah. Click on both links to view the blog posts.

https://leslieslane.wordpress.com/2016/09/11/leslies-leisure-presents-luxury-for-less-in-historic-savannah-georgia/
https://leslieslane.wordpress.com/2015/06/22/june-leslies-lane-featuring-leslies-luxury-living-in-savannah-georgia/

I absolutely love historic Savannah. Whenever I visit, I prefer to stay on world famous River Street or Bay Street. I find the water to be so calming and relaxing. My husband and I stroll along the internationally renowned streets just enjoying the beauty of the city. I really like the hanging moss from the centuries old trees, blooming flowers and historic artifacts of the past. If you are planning a trip to the city and are looking for a great place to stay, there are a number of luxury hotels from which you can choose. Here are a few of my favorites!

The Westin Savannah Harbor Golf Resort and Spa
http://deals.westin.com/Westin-Savannah-Harbor-Hotel-1169/special-offers
The Hyatt Savannah - https://savannah.regency.hyatt.com/en/hotel/offers.html
Savannah Marriott Riverfront
http://www.marriott.com/hotels/hotel-deals/savrf-savannah-marriott-riverfront/

Andaz Savannah - https://savannah.andaz.hyatt.com/en/hotel/offers.html

 **Visit Leopold's Ice Cream (since 1919) I** love the succulent sandwiches and delicious ice cream! https://www.leopoldsicecream.com/.

For places to stay, great restaurants, tours and more, see Visit Savannah website:http://www.visitsavannah.com/.

Use the FREE space below to freestyle!
Grab some colored pencils and doodle, draw, brainstorm, reflect or whatever!

July Leslie's Lane: Featuring Leslie's Leisure in Philadelphia, Pennsylvania

Posted on July 27, 2015, by Leslie's Lane

https://leslieslane.wordpress.com/2015/07/27/
july-leslies-lane-featuring-leslies-luxury-living-
in-philadelphia-pennsylvania/

For the Fourth of July, Tony and I elected to
take a road trip! We thought about it! And
we decided, why not go to the birthplace of
America's independence? We set our sights on
historic Philadelphia, Pennsylvania—a city rich
in history, culture, fine architecture, and remark-
able landmarks! The beautiful hometown of my good friends Tan, Don and
Lanada did not disappoint! We arrived in the midst of the Wawa Welcome
America Philadelphia Celebration! The eight-day festival culminated on July
4 with the largest FREE concert in America featuring The Roots and surprise
guest Cee-lo! I tell you! It was INCREDIBLE!!! As you read this travel piece,
I trust that you find lots of exciting things to do that will help you plan a trip
to the "City of Brotherly Love" in the weeks and months to come.

This was my first time visiting the historic city of Philadelphia. I knew that I
wanted a hotel in the midst of the fun celebrations, interesting attractions, prom-
inent landmarks, and popular restaurants.

Therefore, I went to my favorite search engines,
TripAdvisor and Expedia. There are several
luxury hotels located in this area! I selected the
Le Méridien and an excellent choice it was.
This contemporary hotel is stunningly beautiful! The modern décor blends seamlessly and
elegantly with historical architecture. Every
aspect of the Le Méridien is magnificent.
When making your reservations, it's always a

great idea to ask for a room with a view. I was able to look out at Philadelphia City Hall—one of the most beautiful public buildings I've ever seen.

Now that you've found the perfect hotel that is central to all the surrounding attractions, it's time to go sightseeing! Touring historic Philadelphia was all that I imagined it to be and much more! Tony and I walked the actual halls and grounds that the founding fathers walked. The history books came alive for me as I trekked from place to place! Seeing The Liberty Bell for the first time was an awe-inspiring experience for me. I felt like I was unearthing so much of America's history, and it was so very exciting and exhilarating! If you've visited before, you should rediscover it for the second time! If, like me, you have never been, experience this great culture firsthand! The best thing to do is search the city's official tourism, visitors, or travel sites. For Philadelphia, they are Visit Philadelphia at http://www.visitphilly.com/ and PHL CVB (http://www.discoverphl.com/). They will tell you about all things "Philly"! Find out about hotels, the most popular attractions, the best restaurants, upcoming special events, conventions, meeting space, and more!

Take a Solo, Couples, or Group Retreat to Wondrous Serenbe! It's Heaven on Earth!

https://leslieslane.wordpress.com/2016/07/29/take-a-solo-couples-or-group-retreat-to-wondrous-serenbe-its-heaven-on-earth%E2%80%8F/
Posted on July 29, 2016, by Leslie's Lane

If you've always imagined getting a little closer to heaven, Serenbe is the idyllic place to be. This picturesque, environmentally friendly community is a nurturing place of warmth, relaxation, and serenity. The natural beauty of the landscape is simply stunning. Just envision stepping back in time to a quiet, beautiful, and leisurely pace of living. Whether you're flying solo and need time to rest and relax, are traveling with your significant other and want to reconnect and reignite, or are making reservations for members of a group to get revitalized and revived, Serenbe is the ideal locale.

The Serenbe Inn—Enjoy the luxurious guest accommodations as you relax on the sprawling forty-acre countryside. The nightly room rate includes afternoon tea, evening dessert, and a full country breakfast. Ask about their specials that include shows, plays, or specialty dinners. You can make reservations online at http://serenbeinn. com/. To check into additional savings, try www.tripadvisor.com.

The Duck Inn—In addition to the inn, guests may reserve any of the eighteen striking cottages, homes, townhomes, bungalows, or lofts for nightly stays or extended periods of time. The Duck Inn is one of them. The spacious, multifloor, beautifully contemporary loft provides all that guests need. It features

a full, state-of-the art kitchen; two spacious, private baths; two vibrantly decorated bedrooms; an airy living room leading out to the balcony; a romantic fireplace, and a great dining area. Please click on this link: http://serenbeinn.com/ accommodations/the-duck.

The General Store—For an extra-special treat, take a leisurely stroll to Serenbe's General Store. There you can purchase grocery items, dairy, produce, meats, breads, jams and jellies, gifts, and picnic baskets. The establishment partners with Storico Fresco and Souper Jenny to provide ready-made meals for residents and guests daily. For other great products, see http://www. generalstoreatserenbe.com/

Leslie's Listening!
OK…let's talk! I wanted this book to be interactive. I would love to partner with you as you become inspired, empowered, and informed. Here are a few questions for you to consider as you ponder what you want from this chapter.

How often would you like to travel?

_____

_____

What is your budget?

_____

_____

How will you save?

_____

_____

Are you willing to curtail eating out and put that money in your travel-ONLY piggy bank?

_____

_____

Is there anything that I have not asked that you would like to share?

_____

_____

_____

_____

_____

OK! Let's get to WORK!

Four

Greetings, Beautiful Friends! ☺

We all need information and resources from time to time. As a journalist, my need for resources is perpetual and unending. As I shared in my initial introduction, the need for information requested by my family and friends was the catalyst to my starting my Leslie's Lane blog.

In this chapter, you will find a wealth of knowledge packed in a few pages. That includes: fundraisers, veterans, down-payment assistance for homes, childcare, health care, taxes, and much more.

At the end of the chapter, there are fill-in-the-blank questions to help assist you as you research all subject matter that is vitally important to you and your beautiful family! Thanks so much for your support, and have a great week! Happy Reading and Research!

Sincerely,

Leslie

Can you tell me about resources?

"In my line of work, discounts serve to save money in purchasing material, tools, or gaining estimates for projects. Purchasing tools can often be an expensive proposition. So it helps to know when discounts or deals are available as well as where the best deals can be gained. What I would like to see is the underlying principles of how discounts are sought out. What are steps that I can take that would narrow down my search for an item so that I would get the best deal? Maybe you could address character qualities which are related to discounts. For example, being patient for the best deal, organization, preplanning and other things that are necessary. What are the ways we can personally develop so that we won't settle for the quick and more expensive route?"

—— *Richard "Lewis", a carpenter, wants to know about resources at his disposal.*

Perspective & Words of Advice from *Leslie's Lane: The Book!* Resources Expert

"Business owners who are looking for training or development materials for business or their industry should first create a list of experts who are teaching on the particular subject matter. They should go to each expert's website and check out the free and discounted resources they offer. Each expert usually offers a few free resources such as webinars, cheat sheets, templates etc. that will help the business owner get started. This will also get them on the e-mail list to be the first to hear about and be offered discounted prices for additional material. If the business owner is looking for material to create a product or service, then stalking the discount websites is a good bet, sites such as Amazon and eBay. If they need a large bulk order, places such as Alibaba will have great discounted or wholesale prices."

—— *Maria James, PhD is the Founder and CEO of Pocket of Money, LLC*

Leslie's Lessons—Five Tips at a Glance! Check Out Some of the Best Resources Websites

1. Home—http://www.fha-home-loans.com/down_payment_assistance_programs_fha_loans.htm
2. Childcare—http://www2.ed.gov/about/offices/list/oii/nonpublic/childcare.html
3. Veterans—http://www.blogs.va.gov/VAntage/
4. Childcare—https://www.carelulu.com/
5. Down payment—http://downpaymentresource.com/

Leslie's Litany—Three Books to Read! Check Out Some of the Best Resources Books

1. *The Guide to Buying a House for the Low to Moderate Income Family!* By M.G. West
2. *The Military Advantage: The Military.com Guide to Military and Veterans Benefits* by Terry Howell
3. *The Essential Fundraising Guide: for K-12 Schools* by Stan Levenson

Leslie's Lane The Book!
Expert Info at a Glance!
Company: Pocket of Money, LLC
Website: https://pocketofmoney.com/
Facebook: https://www.facebook.com/PocketofMoneyLLC/?fref=ts
Twitter: @UrPocketofMoney
Instagram: @pocketofmoneyllc

Richard is like many self-employed individuals looking for information at no or low cost. Small business owners can get free resources and online tools with *Business Accelerator also known as Dream Fearlessly.* It's an excellent online publication that I write for. If you are a small-business person, free resources are heaven sent. Please check out this link for lots of info: https://www.dreamfearlessly.com/business-accelerator/. Also, it's a great idea to watch television shows, listen to radio shows, and tune into YouTube videos that offer free advice and DIY info.

From My Big Eyes—My friend and sorority sister Janet created this really cool blog. It features promotions, giveaways, breakfast freebies, movie premieres, and more. Check out the link: http://www.frommybigeyes.com/.

Low-cost Internet for low-income families—The Internet should be available to all people—regardless of income. There are a few organizations providing low-cost service. The links are
www.windstream.com
www.att.com (five-dollar Internet)

How to apply for SNAP—It is just so important that we serve those less fortune and in need. The Supplemental Nutrition Assistance Program (SNAP) does so. Please go to this website: http://www.fns.usda.gov/snap/applicant_recipients/apply.htm. If you don't have a need, pass it along to a family that does.

Our veterans have given so much to us in order for us to live in the land of the free. I'm happy to share this section with so many dedicated men and women. Freebies, discounts, and deals for veterans:
http://militarybenefits.info/veterans-day-discounts-sales-deals-free-meals/
US Department of Veteran Affairs resources for vets:
http://www.blogs.va.gov/VAntage/
The following link has gone viral. There are links to numerous resources for veterans. This is exceptional information:
http://www.cpvva.org/BENEFITS.HTML

Special thanks to my real estate friends Jenice Brinkley of Brinkley Realty Group—http://www.brinkleyrealtygroup.com/ and Shindana Johnson of Keller Williams Realty—http://www.shinwinsrealty.com/buyer-info/. They often make me aware of free homebuyers' seminars featuring down-payment-assistance programs. Check it out at:
http://www.fha-home-loans.com/down_payment_assistance_programs_fha_loans.htm

Childcare resources—Young mothers and couples sometimes need a hand with childcare. Whether you're working or in school, you can be assured your child is in good hands in a reputable day care.

Seven sources to help pay for childcare:
https://www.care.com/a/7-sources-to-help-pay-for-child-care-1413918826744
Childcare grant info:
http://www2.ed.gov/about/offices/list/oii/nonpublic/childcare.html
Free and low-cost day care for single moms:
http://www.singlemotherinfo.com/free-daycare/
Get help paying for childcare:
http://www.pathwaysla.org/en/parent-resources/get-help-paying
Free or low-cost childcare programs:
http://www.4c.org/parent/needing_help/index.html
Subsidized childcare in New York:
http://www.dccnyinc.org/view/page/subsidized_child_care_

If you lack funds and need assistance with preparing your tax returns, check out the link below. Further, if you owe the government, it's possible some of your debt can be forgiven.
Offer in compromise:
https://www.irs.gov/individuals/offer-in-compromise-1
FREE tax preparation:

https://www.irs.gov/individuals/free-tax-return-preparation-for-you-by-volunteers

FREE workshops on home improvement—Are you handy with a hammer? Do you like the do-it-yourself options? Well, check out free workshops at Home Depot. Lowe's even has free workshops for kids called Lowe's Build and Grow. Be sure to check your neighborhood home improvement store to see if they have workshops as well.
http://workshops.homedepot.com/workshops/home
https://lowesbuildandgrow.com/

Thanks to Maria James for this supplemental information to what I have included! Financial literacy information tailored for veterans can be found at a number of blogs and sites, such as Veterans Plus: http://www.veteransplus.org/, Debt.org: https://www.debt.org/veterans/, The Military Wallet: http://themilitarywallet.com/category/military-money/, USA Cares: http://www.usacares.org/, and Military Money Matters: http://www.military-money-matters.com/. For assistance paying for childcare, individuals should check with their state and county social services programs. Parents should also try out the site CareLuLu: https://www.carelulu.com/. Individuals looking to buy a home should take a look at Down Payment Resource: http://downpaymentresource.com/, which will help locate programs that can assist with the down payment.

Fundraisers for your organization
Whether it's your school, church, kids' athletic, booster club or another organization, fundraisers help raise a much-needed cash infusion for your respective programs. As a kid growing up, I cannot tell you how many Krispy Kreme Donuts, Byrd's Famous Cookies, and World's Finest Chocolate candy bars we sold as fundraisers. It was a lot! They were really cool fundraisers. Chick-fil-A Cow Calendars are simply awesome as fundraisers. You get a card that has a FREE item every month. We sold so many of them when my hubby was a Chick-fil-A operator! The organization raises money, and the purchaser has

something tangible for the whole year! Not to mention that the freebies in the cow calendar far exceed the amount they paid!

Chick-fil-A Cow Calendar Fundraisers—http://www.chick-fil-a.com/Kids/Local

Krispy Kreme Fundraising—http://krispykreme.com/Fundraising

ABC Fundraising—http://www.abcfundraising.com/

Little Caesars Pizza—http://www.pizzakit.com/

World's Finest Chocolate—https://www.worldsfinestchocolate.com/

Use the FREE space below to freestyle!
Grab some colored pencils and doodle, draw, brainstorm, reflect or whatever!

Leslie's Listening!
OK…let's talk! I wanted this book to be interactive. I would love to partner with you as you become inspired, empowered, and informed. Here are a few questions for you to consider as you ponder what you want from this chapter.

Can you name five specific resources you and your family need now to be empowered?

Resource 1
_____

Resource 2
_____

Resource 3
_____

Resource 4
_____

Resource 5
_____

How will you go about obtaining these resources?
1. _____
_____
2. _____
_____
3. _____
_____
4. _____
_____
5. _____
_____

Is there anything that I have not asked that you would like to share?

_____

_____

_____

_____

_____

OK! Let's get to WORK!

Five

Discounts

Greetings, Beautiful Friends! ☺

Everybody loves a discount, right? I rarely pay full price for anything! I mean…why pay 100 percent when you can pay fifty cents, twenty-five cents, or ten cents on the dollar! This chapter shares how you can get coupons for grocery shopping and discounts on meals, hotels, websites, restaurants, services, products, AARP, Amazon (70 percent off), membership clubs, auctions, outlets, and more.

Also, if you like designer purses, shoes, and clothing, you can go to outlet stores that provide 50 percent off on a regular basis and from time to time, up to 70 percent off, 80 percent off, or 90 percent off. You don't want to pay department-store prices if you are willing to drive a little to an outlet store and save like crazy!

Just a little research and legwork will save you a lot of money! Check out all the links in this chapter to get you started. At the end of the chapter, quiz yourself on various ways you want to get discounts. Thanks so much for your support, and have a great week! Happy Reading and Research!

Sincerely,

Leslie

Can you tell me about discounts?

"I enjoy having information about cost-saving resources. It is important to me so that I can do comparison shopping. This way I can get the 'best bang for my buck', get even more products and save money. It makes for a win-win situation.

I'd like to know about quantity (how many products are available for the best price) in order to make the most informed decision(s). I want to know about quality. The products need to be of good quality and substance for longevity and endurance. Can you tell me about comparing online shopping to shopping in person in a mall, grocery store or boutique, etc? I have become a HUGE fan of online shopping. I find that some of the products offered are not found in the stores. Shopping can be done within the confines of your home without giving thought of getting dressed, parking and security issues. The pros far outweigh the cons."

— Rowena Dennard, a retired music educator, wants to know about the best discounts.

Perspective & Words of Advice
from *Leslie's Lane: The Book!*
Discounts Expert

"To determine how to compare discounts for online versus shopping in person, there are a few apps you can use. You can use Retailmenot. It will help to show you coupons that are available. You can use Ebates. It offers cash back when you buy anything. I bought a trip on Groupon. My last favorite one—Honey—is great. You download it on your computer. Every time you go online, Honey will comb the Internet and find codes for your purchase that you do not have yourself. To get quality or upscale products at substantially discounted prices, you can shop at high-end stores. If you shop off season, that is one of the best ways to find quality goods at discount prices. You can find something at 60 to 80 percent off. You don't have to forgo quality for price. People tend to get frustrated when looking for discounts. It takes a little patience. But it is worth it in the end. There is always some kind of discount available."

— Tiffany "The Budgetnista" Aliche is the owner of the Budgetnista and author of several bestselling books.

Leslie's Lessons—Five Tips at a Glance! Check Out Some of the Best Discounts Websites

1. www.groupon.com
2. www.livingsocial.com
3. www.scoutmob.com
4. www.restaurant.com
5. www.retailmenot.com

Leslie's Litany—Three Books to Read! Check Out Some of the Best Discounts Books

1. *The Smart Girl's Guide to Discount Shopping* by Sher Bailey and Liz Nieman
2. *Cheap and Functional DIY Box Set (6 in 1)* by Calvin Hale, Parker Harris, Ronda Powell, Carrie Bishop, and Vanessa Riley
3. *Five Star Living on a Two-Star Budget* by Margaret Feinberg and Natalie Nichols Gillespie

Leslie's Lane The Book!
Expert Info at a Glance!
Company: The Budgetnista
Website: http://thebudgetnista.com/
Facebook: https://www.facebook.com/budgetnista/?fref=ts
Twitter: @Budgetnista
Instagram: @thebudgetnista

I have great idea about coupons! When I worked at the FBI, we started a coupon basket. You should do one at work, home, church, and so on. It goes like this: take the coupons you want; bring the ones you don't! So at home, clip all the coupons. Bring the ones you don't want to work, and leave them in the basket. Then, take the coupons from the basket that you do use! It worked really well for us for years! I wonder if they are still doing it…hmm.

Of course, now everything is on the Internet. It is so convenient. Many companies will allow you to print out two manufacturers' coupons. Check out these sites. Some even give you cash back.
http://www.savingstar.com
www.upromise.com
www.coupons.com
www.smartsource.com
www.redplum.com

Thanks to the Beautiful One—my daughter, Antasha—for this one. Honey. com is relatively new to me. It's revolutionary! It is a Google Chrome extension that combs the Internet for you. It finds and applies discounts and coupon codes. Check it out at www.joinhoney.com. It just so happens that Honey is the Budgetnista's new favorite too!

You can eat at many of the restaurants for at least half off! I like to have a monthly mother-son luncheon and mother-daughter luncheon. Antasha and I like to go to restaurants that allow us to use certificates for at least half off. Many people's budgets tend to be stretched at the end of payday. You've paid the house note or rent and all the utility bills. Yet…you want to go out to eat. You should be able to enjoy yourself without breaking the bank. These sites are a cost-saving way to do just that. Go on. Enjoy some time with your family and friends.

1. www.groupon.com
2. www.livingsocial.com

3. www.scoutmob.com
4. www.restaurant.com
5. www.bitehunter.com
6. www.savored.com
7. www.opentable.com
8. www.citysearch.com
9. www.eatdrinkdeals.com
10. www.retailmenot.com

Great sites for discounts—These sites are some of my favorites, each for different reasons. AARP (www.aarp.com) is one of the best clubs in the world! As I shared, I've been waiting to join this elite group for a long time! As soon as Tony turned fifty a few years ago, I jumped right in. You see, regardless of your spouse's age, he or she can be a member too. AARP offers discounts on travel, insurance, automotive, financial, shopping, services, and more.

"Triple A," as it is affectionately called, is far more than a roadside assistance group. It offers discounts on insurance, travel, hotels, and 150,000 retail locations. Check them out at www.aaa.com.

I love Amazon! I especially like the 70 percent off. Just Google "Amazon 70 percent off" or go to Amazon (www.amazon.com) and search. Please don't forget to sign up for Amazon Smile. A portion of what you spend goes to your favorite charity. Mine is Berean Community Development Corporation. It is part of Berean Christian Church, of which I am a member.

Living on the Cheap (http://livingonthecheap.com/) is really cool. It's in Atlanta and provides exceptional information.

Retailmenot (www.retailmenot.com) is awesome! Just download the app to your phone. When you are in a restaurant or retail, automotive, electronic, or furniture store, just pull it up and use the coupons. It also works on events and attractions.

I've just discovered these. Check them out to see if you like them.
Freebies2Deals—http://freebies2deals.com/
Slickdeals.net—http://slickdeals.net/
Overstock.com—www.overstock.com

It's always nice being a part of an exclusive club! Especially when you get discounts! Just go to these websites to see if you are part of an organization that qualifies.
www.samsclub.com
www.costco.com
Employee Discount Club—http://www.employeediscountclub.com/
Start a Discount Club with Access Development—http://www.accessdevelopment.com/discount-membership-clubs/

Want discounts on appliances and electronics? Try outlet stores! Tony and I have been going to outlet stores for years. We have mostly gone to the Sears Outlet in Tucker, Georgia. We have been very pleased with our appliances. Feel free to check out these sites:
Sears Outlet—up to 80 percent off items—http://www.searsoutlet.com/
Whirlpool Outlet—http://outlet.whirlpool.com/
GE Outlet Store—https://www.geoutletstore.com
Wholesale Appliance Center—https://www.wholesaleappliancecenter.com/
Discount Electronics—http://www.tigerdirect.com/
Best Buy Outlet for Clearance and Refurbished Electronics—http://www.bestbuy.com/site/misc/outlet-refurbished-clearance
Geek's Discount—http://www.geeks.com/products.asp?cat=CON

There are several furniture outlet stores we've frequented. Please check out these to see if they work for you. You can also check local outlets in your area.
Rooms to Go Outlet—http://www.roomstogo-outlet.com/
American Family Furniture—http://www.americanfreight.us/
Underpriced Furniture—http://www.underpricedfurniture.com/

Great prices on luxury items—Why pay full price when you don't have to do so? I like getting discounts of 25 percent, 50 percent, or 75 percent off. Luxury items are no different. In fact, if designer items are not at least 60 percent off, I typically will not buy them. If you like designer and luxury items and refuse to pay the full price, check out links to auctions and premium outlet stores. Before you do so, check out my *Black Enterprise* article "How to Look Like a Millionaire Without Breaking the Bank" at http://www.blackenterprise.com/mag/living-the-glamorous-life/. Also take a look at these sites:

Luxury Car Outlet—http://www.luxurycaroutlet.com/
Government Auctions—https://www.usa.gov/buy-from-government
Government Fleet Sales—https://autoauctions.gsa.gov/GSAAutoAuctions/
US Government Auctions—http://usgovernmentauctions.net/
Government Auctions and Foreclosures—http://www.governmentauctions.org/
US Marshal's Auction—http://www.usmarshals.gov/assets/sales.htm
US Department of Treasury Auction (IRS)—https://www.treasury.gov/services/Pages/auctions_index.aspx
Home Foreclosure Auctions—https://www.auction.com/residential/foreclosures
HUD Home Foreclosure Auctions—http://www.hudhomesusa.org/

Whenever I get a chance to go to a clothing outlet store, I jump at the chance. I go to the North Georgia Premium Outlets, just outside of Atlanta. I like the premium outlets in Orlando too! My favorite shops are Michael Kors, Coach, and Nike. Tony has a special affinity for Tommy Hilfiger!

Premium Outlets—http://www.premiumoutlets.com/
Miromar Outlets—http://www.miromaroutlets.com/
Tanger Outlets—http://www.tangeroutlet.com/

Join a hair club—Does your hairstylist offer discounts? I go to Don Janelle Unisex Hair Salon, and I absolutely love my stylists, Stephanie Janelle Bryant and Donna London. They are a great mother-daughter tandem. They have the "VIP Hair Club." The price is great. The four different packages are tailor-made for you. I pay half of what I would pay if I weren't in the club. Check out their website - http://www.donjanelle.com/. If you are outside of Atlanta, ask the stylists in your city if they offer something comparable.

Thanks to my BFF (Best Friend Forever) Lisa Kirk for this information. Did you know that you can go to beauty, spa, or nail schools in your area to have services at a discount price? Just search the Internet to find locales that suite your fancy. Here are a few examples:

Get Discounts on Hair Services at Beauty Schools
Empire Beauty School
http://www.empire.edu/guest-services/hair-services

Get Discounts on Spa Services at Spa Schools
The Spa at Elaine Sterling Institute
http://spaatesi.com/

Get Discounts on Nail Services at Nail Schools
Nail Logic—The Institute of Nail Technology
http://www.naillogicinstitute.com/nail-services.html

Thanks to The Handsome One – my son, Jay – for this info. Before paying more than you have to for household items, look for $1.00 items at Dollar Tree, Family Dollar and Walmart.

> "One of the most prolific ways to secure high quality fash-
> ions in your wardrobe is to consistently indulge yourself in
> the practice of thrifting. Thrifting is not simply defined as
> thrift store hopping. No, it is actually a way of shopping all
> together. For example, going to stores that sell designer fash-
> ions at clearance prices (H&M, Marshall's, TJ Maxx) and
> then complementing these items with a "big ticket item"
> from a thrift store. For 2015/2016's winter season, I found

*a vintage $250 polish designed, gray trench coat at a price
of only $26.50! What a steal! This is an item that will stand
the test of time, holds lots of utility and vitality as well as
just simply being fabulous! Get started thrifting today!"*
— Bryson Jones, My Godson.

**Use the FREE space below to freestyle!
Grab some colored pencils and doodle, draw, brainstorm,
reflect or whatever!**

Leslie's Listening!

OK…let's talk! I wanted this book to be interactive. I would love to partner with you as you become inspired, empowered, and informed. Here are a few questions for you to consider as you ponder what you want from this chapter.

Are you willing to comb the Internet for desired information?

_____

_____

Do you like finer things in life, and if so, are you willing to research outlets in cities you're visiting?

_____

_____

Are you willing to try new restaurants to get at least half off?

_____

_____

How do you feel about attending auctions to purchase vehicles with cash?

_____

_____

What type of discounts would you like to have?
1. Desired discount: _____
2. Desired discount: _____
3. Desired discount: _____
4. Desired discount: _____
5. Desired discount: _____

Is there anything that I have not asked that you would like to share?

_____

_____

_____

_____

_____

OK! Let's get to WORK!

Six

Financial Aid: Scholarships, Grants, Loans, and Loan Forgiveness

Greetings, Beautiful Friends! ☺

Having two children—Antasha and Jay—who have gone to college and want to continue their secondary education, I know a little something about financial aid. I know a great deal about financing one's education too! I personally began my studies at Savannah State University (Go SSU Tigers), completed my undergrad degree at Georgia State University (Go GSU Panthers) with a degree in Journalism, and received a Master of Arts in Christian Education and a Master of Divinity from Luther Rice College and Seminary (Jesus Rocks!).

I'm excited about sharing this chapter on scholarships, which also includes grants, student loans, and other forms of aid. I don't think it's ever too soon to start researching information on scholarships for your children. Likewise, even if you don't anticipate going back to school for several years, you can do your research now.

At the end of this chapter, feel free to answer questions about where you want to go, whether you want to stay on or off campus, what you want to spend, whether you want to go to private or public school, and so forth and so on. Thanks so much for your support, and have a great week! Happy Reading and Research!

Sincerely,

Leslie

Can you tell me about financial aid?

"Both of my children were blessed as we didn't have to pay one cent for their college education. I want everyone to have the opportunity to go to college. I want all parents to understand that his or her child must maintain an intense focus on their academics and know how to write why they should receive a scholarship. Extracurricular and community service is important, and one's behavior in and out of the school environment is just as important and can determine if one receives a scholarship. I would like to know the academic criteria for scholarships so that I can be in a position to help others. My husband, Buck Godfrey, was the high school football coach at Southwest DeKalb High School for thirty years. He felt that all of his players and managers had a strong desire to attend college. He obtained scholarships for 270 of them. Of those students, 241 of them graduated."

—— *Joyce Godfrey, known as "Mama G", is a retired grandmother who wants to educate her entire community on scholarships.*

Perspective & Words of Advice
from *Leslie's Lane: The Book!*
Scholarships Expert

"Academics are important when securing scholarships that are based off merit. However, there are many scholarships students may be eligible for outside of academics. For instance, Athletic, Leadership, Internship, Interest/Major scholarships are not based off of academic performance. Last year, over 100 million dollars in scholarships went unclaimed. Therefore, it is imperative to encourage students to apply for scholarships/grants as it will minimize debt and default rates. There are many ways to secure grants and scholarships nationally and locally. Students may use various search engines to find scholarships. There are scholarships for almost any and everything. Yet, you must do the research. Many students like to utilize Fastweb, College Board, Chegg and Scholarships.com. However, there is also a new app called Scholly that narrows down scholarships that you may qualify for based off of your profile. Also, scholarships can be found by speaking with guidance counselors and financial advisors as well as visiting career centers and local organizations (i.e. churches, non-profits, debutante, sororities and fraternities)."

—— *Jessica Brown is the Founder and*
CEO of College Gurl —— "The 101 of Paying for College" website.

Leslie's Lessons—Five Tips at a Glance! Check Out Some of the Best Financial-Aid Websites

1. https://fafsa.ed.gov/
2. www.fastweb.com
3. www.studentloans.gov
4. www.finaid.org
5. www.petersons.com

Leslie's Litany—Three Books to Read! Check Out Some of the Best Financial-Aid Books

1. *The Financial Aid Handbook* by Carol Stack and Ruth Vedvik
2. *The Ultimate Scholarship Book 2017* by Gen Tanabe and Kelly Tanabe
3. *Student Loan Forgiveness and Loan Repayment Programs* by Congressional Research Service

Leslie's Lane The Book!
Expert Info at a Glance!
Company: College Gurl
Website: http://www.collegegurl.com/
Facebook: https://www.facebook.com/collegegurljb/?fref=ts
Twitter: @collegegurljb
Instagram: @collegegurljb

Tony and I have always felt that education is the "great equalizer." Higher education is so important. But more importantly, young people and even older adults going back to school should have access to an affordable education. Are you ready to go back to school? Well, let's do this!!!! Please check out these great links. But first, go to the FAFSA site to submit your free application.

Begin by submitting a FREE application for federal student loans and grants: https://fafsa.ed.gov/

Check out this really popular site for financial aid!
www.unigo.com

Forty-six pages of scholarships for new Americans and minorities:
http://www.dfwinternational.org/resource_center/Scholarship_Guide.pdf

2016 college scholarships:
http://www.fastweb.com/college-scholarships/articles/the-2016-scholarships

One hundred scholarships:
http://www.thepennyhoarder.com/100-college-scholarships/

Fifty great college scholarships:
http://superscholar.org/50-great-college-scholarships/

Scholarships for international students:
http://www.internationalscholarships.com/

Fun and unique scholarships for high-school students:
https://www.pdx.edu/ubets/sites/www.pdx.edu.ubets/files/Scholarships%20 for%20Students.pdf

Scholarships for high-school seniors and college undergraduates:
https://www.uakron.edu/dotAsset/4b6a3052-f4c1-4332-974b- 004759d0abd8.pdf

National directory of scholarships and internships for Asian Americans/Pacific Islanders:
http://www.aast.umd.edu/wp-content/uploads/2012/11/2013-2015-Scholarship-Directory-Web.pdf

Scholarships for US students studying abroad:
http://www.nafsa.org/Explore_International_Education/For_Students/U_S__Study_Abroad_Scholarships_and_Grants_List/

Study-abroad scholarships:
https://www.scholarships.com/financial-aid/college-scholarships/scholarships-by-type/study-abroad-scholarships/

API study-abroad scholarships:
https://www.apistudyabroad.com/students/financial-information/scholarships/

Grants for low-income students:
http://www.collegescholarships.org/grants/low-income.htm

States offering FREE community college:
http://www.huffingtonpost.com/entry/free-community-college-already-happening_us_565b968de4b079b2818ab7de

Info on FREE community college legislation:
http://www.ncsl.org/research/education/free-community-college.aspx

Georgia student grants for college:
http://www.collegescholarships.org/grants/states/georgia.htm

Scholarships and grants for single mothers:
https://www.scholarships.com/financial-aid/college-scholarships/scholarships-by-type/college-scholarships-and-grants-for-single-mothers/

Scholarships for women and single mothers:
https://www.salliemae.com/plan-for-college/scholarships/scholarships-for-women-and-single-mothers/

Check out why 2.9 billion dollars in FREE college money has gone unclaimed:
http://www.fastweb.com/financial-aid/articles/over-2-point-nine-billion-in-free-college-money-unclaimed-by-students-why

An app to help students get FREE money for college:
http://www.forbes.com/sites/annefield/2014/02/14/an-app-to-help-students-get-free-money-for-college/#1c249a327ef0

Types of grants and scholarships:
https://studentaid.ed.gov/sa/types/grants-scholarships

Twenty ways to get federal money for college:
http://www.bankrate.com/finance/college-finance/20-ways-to-get-federal-money-for-college-1.aspx

MALDEF scholarship resource guide:
http://www.maldef.org/assets/pdf/2016-2017_MALDEF_Scholarship_List.pdf

FREE education for Georgia students seeking a technical degree!
The HOPE Grant program is for students seeking a technical certification or diploma, regardless of the student's high-school grade-point average or graduation date. For more information, please review the HOPE Grant regulations. Go to this link and search for "Georgia Tuition Equalization Grant." Plus, you can find info on other Georgia scholarships including the HOPE Scholarship at www.gacollege411.org.

Links on student loan forgiveness—Did you know there are opportunities to have your loan forgiven? Check out a few websites and articles detailing how you can do so:

http://www.forgetstudentloandebt.com/student-loan-relief-programs/
http://www.usnews.com/education/blogs/student-loan-ranger/2015/02/11/
what-obamas-2016-budget-proposal-means-for-student-borrowers
https://www.congress.gov/bill/114th-congress/senate-bill/2099
http://studentdebtcenter.org/student-loan-forgiveness/
http://www.magnifymoney.com/blog/college-students-and-recent-grads/
get-student-loan-forgiven1190167365

**Use the FREE space below to freestyle!
Grab some colored pencils and doodle, draw, brainstorm,
reflect or whatever!**

Leslie's Listening!

OK…let's talk! I wanted this book to be interactive. I would love to partner with you as you become inspired, empowered, and informed. Here are a few questions for you to consider as you ponder what you want from this chapter.

Have you filled out the FAFSA?

_____

_____

If not, when will you do so?

_____

_____

What would you like to study?

_____

_____

Where would you like to go?

_____

_____

Will it be a technical, two-year, or four-year school?

_____

_____

Will it be a private or public school?

_____

_____

Is there anything that I have not asked that you would like to share?

_____

_____

OK! Let's get to WORK!

Seven

Free and Discounted Medical and Dental Services

Greetings, Beautiful Friends! ☺

Of all the chapters in this book, I think this one tugs at my heartstrings the most. I guess it's because I feel helpless, and it's difficult for me to do anything about it. It hurts me that so many people I know are uninsured or underinsured. They don't have dental insurance, and even when they have some form of medical insurance, it simply isn't enough. Plus, many can't afford the price of prescriptions.

President Barack H. Obama passed the Affordable Care Act (ACA). It is actually the Patient Protection and Affordable Care Act (PPACA). Please check out the website on how it works. Additionally, peruse links to free and discount medical resources available to you and your family.

Seniors particularly have difficulty with dental care and dentures. Many people cannot afford prescription drugs. There are organizations, including pharmaceutical companies, that offer free and low-cost drugs for them.

At the end of the chapter, you can ponder how you can tap into these resources by answering various questions. I trust that you find this helpful.

Have a great day! Thanks so much for your support, and have a great week! Happy Reading and Research!

Sincerely,

Leslie

Can you tell me about FREE and discount medical care?
"With the high cost of healthcare, every discount you can get is a cost savings to your pocketbook. I want to ask this question for me, my family and anyone that may be in need such as my church members and friends. Are there services that are free and discounted that can be used in addition to your medical insurance?"

— Trudie E. Carmichael is a contracting officer for a local government and wants to know about discount healthcare for those in need.

Perspective & Words of Advice
from *Leslie's Lane: The Book!*
Discount Healthcare Expert

"Many people may qualify for coverage through Medicaid and the Children's Health Insurance Program. If for some reason you do not qualify, contact your local community health center. The amount you pay depends upon your income. The community health centers are located in both urban and rural areas. There are prescription assistance programs that are known as indigent drug programs or charitable drug programs. There are many dental schools associated with local colleges and universities that offer free dental treatment. Many of these programs may inquire about your income and assets in order to qualify you for help."

— Dr. Annette Boone-Hicks is a Doctor of Chiropractic and Owner of The Boone Clinic, P.C.

Leslie's Lessons—Five Tips at a Glance! Check Out Some of the Best Health-Care Websites

1. http://www.freeclinics.com/
2. http://www.pparx.org
3. http://www.new-eyes.org/source-of-free-eye-exams/
4. http://www.seniorliving.org/healthcare/free-dental-care/
5. www.worldental.org/dental-schools-affordable-free-denistry

Leslie's Litany—Three Books to Read! Check Out Some of the Best Health-Care Books

1. *Hard Times Superbook 7: Free and Low Cost Medical Care & Drugs* by Tony Kelrat
2. *Free Stuff for Women's Health, Fitness and Nutrition* by Matthew Lesko
3. *It Pays to Be a Senior* by the Editors of FC&A Publishing

Leslie's Lane The Book!
Expert Info at a Glance!
Company: The Boone Clinic
Website: N/A
Facebook: https://www.facebook.com/thebooneclinicpc
Twitter: @thebooneclinic
Instagram: N/A

Wow! I was on a conference call with President Barack Obama last year! He discussed open enrollment! I am honored to have been invited to be a part of it with him! He invited only five thousand of us throughout the nation to join his call in listen-only mode. He first thanked us for all we do in our communities. That was a nice pat on the back! He then got down to business! He shared that health care open enrollment was going on at the time. He asked that we pass the word and encourage everyone to go to the Healthcare.gov website. When you get an opportunity, research to find out just how you can get yourself and your family covered.

Are you a senior in need of FREE or low-cost dental service? Check out this info: http://www.seniorliving.org/healthcare/free-dental-care/
Affordable dentures:
http://www.affordabledentures.com/search/state/ga

Free dentures:
http://grantsguys.com/free-dentures/

National Council on Aging:
https://www.ncoa.org/economic-security/benefits/other-benefits/dental/

Nineteen FREE services for seniors and their caregivers:
https://www.agingcare.com/Articles/free-services-for-seniors-or-caregivers-156443.htm

FREE dental care:
http://dentallifeline.org/?gclid=CICOqcbB-swCFUQjgQodj8wKOg

Free and low-cost medical clinics:
http://www.needymeds.org/free_clinics.taf?gclid=CKOfpJfC-swCFUc2gQodzcMOaw

Where to find low-cost dental care—Health and Human Services:
http://www.hhs.gov/answers/health-care/where-can-i-find-low-cost-dental-care/index.html

Blue Ridge free dental care:
http://www.blueridgefreedentalclinic.org/
Free or reduced-cost dental services in Georgia—more than twenty-five counties, colleges providing dental services, Medicaid referral, CMO, and more:
http://med.emory.edu/CDE/services/free_reduced_cost_dental_services.html

FREE clinics:
http://www.freeclinics.com/cit/ga-atlanta
http://www.freeclinics.com/

National Association of FREE and Charitable Clinics
http://www.nafcclinics.org/clinics/search

Low-cost health care in your community:
https://www.healthcare.gov/community-health-centers/
FREE or low-cost health care:
https://www.nlm.nih.gov/services/freemedcare_int.html

FREE glasses and eye exams:
http://www.allaboutvision.com/eye-exam/free-exam.htm

FREE or low-cost eye exams:
http://www.new-eyes.org/source-of-free-eye-exams/

FREE medications from select stores and vendors:
Thanks to the Beautiful One—my daughter Antasha—for this one! You can get free antibiotics, high-blood-pressure medicine, and diabetes medication from Publix! http://www.publix.com/pharmacy-wellness/pharmacy/pharmacy-services/free-medication-program How cool is that?!

Partnership for Prescription Assistance can help you. They have more than twenty-five hundred brand-name or generic prescriptions. You may be able to receive free or low-cost prescriptions. Call 888-4PPA-NOW or visit http://www.pparx.org. Check out these other sites as well.
NeedyMeds.org
RXAssist.org

For social services, see www.govbenefits.com. They have easy online access to government assistance for childcare, counseling, education, health care, HIV/AIDS, food and nutrition, and more. There are FREE and low-cost services for the legally blind and other disabled citizens. Please go to www.disability.gov.

You can also go to the following websites:
www.healthcare.gov/community-health-centers
www.needhelppayingbills.com/html/get_free_health_care.html
www.hrsa.gov/gethealthcare/index.html
www.consumer.ftc.gov/articles/0165-discount-plan

Thanks Dr. Boone-Hicks for this info! Life University offers chiropractic health and wellness care through the Community Outreach Chiropractic Clinic. The services provided include chiropractic care, digital imaging, functional kinesiology, health-care classes, and nutritional counseling. The Community Outreach is open to the public. The contact number is 770-426-2946. The websites are www.life.edu. (chiropractic care)
www.healthcare.gov/community-health-centers (chiropractic, medical, and dental care)

Many dental schools associated with local colleges and universities offer free dental treatment. The programs may want to inquire about your income and assets to qualify you based on your financial status and to see whether you are eligible for the state help. You can find more information on these sites:
www.identalhub.com/article_free-dental-work-494.aspx
www.worldental.org/dental-schools-affordable-free-denistry.

Leslie's Listening!
OK…let's talk! I wanted this book to be interactive. I would love to partner with you as you become inspired, empowered, and informed. Here are a few questions for you to consider as you ponder what you want from this chapter.

Do you have health coverage? If not, how will you go about getting it?

_____

_____

If you have health coverage, do you have enough?

_____

_____

Will your income allow for additional assistance?

_____

_____

Are you a senior? What are your needs?

_____

_____

Do you have small children? What are your needs?

_____

_____

Is there anything that I have not asked that you would like to share?

_____

_____

_____

_____

OK! Let's get to WORK!

Eight

PURSUE YOUR PASSION! CREATING THE JOB OF
YOUR DREAMS!

Greetings, Beautiful Friends! ☺
I absolutely love this chapter! Question: If money were no factor and you had everything you needed, what would be the job of your dreams?! Are you ready to determine your destiny? What about chasing the fulfilling career of your choice? Think about how you can create the job of your dreams and pursue your passion.

I shared my own life experiences in chapter 1. I feel like it's great to be content, but not to be complacent. I had a good job with the FBI. But something in my heart wanted more. And when my little girl Antasha, awakened that longing in my heart, I sprang into action.

This chapter is twofold. You get great info on starting your dream career. Plus, I have something special for writers. At the end of the chapter, there will be several engaging questions to help you think about how to pursue your passion. But remember, don't quit your day job until you have replaced that income. Thanks so much for your support, and have a great week! Happy Reading and Research!

Sincerely,

Leslie

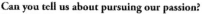

Can you tell us about pursuing our passion?

"I would like to pursue my passion by creating a blog for my daily inspirational messages. I think that it's important for me to continue to reach and uplift people in a non-threatening manner and fulfill my purpose. Having a blog is a great start for me. I could see myself selling a book with daily messages, journals, pens, calendars, etc. with my logo and messages. Can you tell me about blog creation, web design, logos, marketing, seminars, etc.?

— *Kerry V. Anderson works in accounts receivable and inspires others with daily Facebook posts.*

"I would love to pursue my passions. One of my passions is to sing/dance/act in order to become famous because I am very talented. It is better to start pursuing my passion with a little background information. Can you provide it?"

— *Fred Anderson IV is Kerry's son and a high school senior who wants to promote his talents.*

Perspective & Words of Advice
from *Leslie's Lane: The Book!*
Your Passion Experts

"You know when it's time to break out and follow your dream or mission in life when you become very unhappy doing what you don't love. When you do something that you love, you can produce better products and services because it comes from the heart!"

— *Stephanie Janelle Bryant is the Co-Owner of Don Janelle Unisex Hair Spa.*

"To start your own blog, just write what you know. That includes things that interest and concern the client. Emphasize more. Explain the fine details that you can't place in the website. To create a free blog or website, go to Wordpress. Contact Yahoo, Google or other site to ask questions. Go to free workshops or join Meetup groups such as Wordpress Meetup to get info from others. You know you have a passion when what you do is as easy as breathing. Sometimes people will help you along the way and nudge you. My husband at the time told me, 'You love doing this. You should go to school for it.' I was just doing it for fun. That's the catalyst I needed. Be focused on your dream and follow it. It is not a straight road. It is a journey. It has lots of curves, twists and turns. But you have to be willing to follow the curves to get to where you want to go."

— *Donna London is the Co-Owner of Don Janelle Unisex Hair Spa.*

Leslie's Lessons—Five Tips at a Glance!—Check Out Some of the Pursue Your Passion, Follow Your Dreams, and Start a Business Websites

1. www.lifehack.org
2. www.sba.gov
3. www.entrepreneur.com
4. www.backstage.com
5. www.franchise.org

Leslie's Litany—Three Books to Read!—Check Out Some of the Best Pursue Your Passion, Follow Your Dreams, and Start a Business Books

1. *Vital Signs: The Nature and Nurture of Passion* by Gregg Levoy
2. *Put Your Dream to the Test* by John Maxwell
3. *The Art of the Start 2.0* by Guy Kawasaki

Leslie's Lane The Book!
Expert Info at a Glance!
Company: Don Janelle Unisex Hair Salon
Website: http://donjanelle.com/
Facebook: https://www.facebook.com/Don-Janelle-Hair-Salon-51681143505/
?fref=ts
Twitter: @donjanelle
Instagram: @donjanelle

As you seek to pursue your passion, or create the job of your dreams, the first thing I would encourage you to do is select accountability/encouragement partners. I do this every few years or so. I find that they help keep me focused and motivated! They have inspired me so! Please find a few things they had to say about choosing these special people in your life! You can also get a great visual of how I feel about each of them surrounding me with love in the beach photo. In the photo, I was actually at the Beach Cove Resort in Myrtle Beach. My daughter, Antasha snapped the photo.

I'm so glad that my Soror, Friend, and other Sister introduced me to the world of "accountability partners." It is important to help others you trust and love to follow through with their dreams and goals. This is important not only in a marriage, but in all your relationships (family, friends, job, church, social groups, exercise, and so forth).
—Dr. Tan Goodjiones Marilla, My Sorority Sister

It's important to have an accountability partner to ensure your vision stays on course. In times of feeling defeat, you have a support system to relight your fire. I was happy to support my sister in the decision to spread her wings and soar through the "not now" moments and turn those moments into "yes" moments.
—Natalie F. Reese, My Sister

It is important to have someone to encourage you because as we reach for goals, sometimes we may get weary along the way. They can help build us up to keep pressing until we reach our goals. I feel Leslie has grown in so many ways. Not just as a result of my influence, but the influence of Christ in both our lives.
—Alzena Anderson, My Friend

An accountability partner serves as a trusted individual, providing guidance and honest feedback. You should have someone who

encourages your goals in life, because encouragement is what we all require for our overall growth and development. Encouraging and supporting our loved ones is the ultimate expression of love.
—Sybil Jones, My Cousin

It is important to have an accountability partner because that person can help you reach your full potential. He/she helps give you that extra push to keep going when you want to give up, helps to keep you focused, and to keep your priorities in order. At the end of the day, that's what life is all about…being there for each other.
—Cheryl Cross, My Sorority Sister

An accountability partner helps keep you committed and focused on your goals. It is important to have individuals in life who motivate you, provide guidance, and support you to make sure you stay on track and reach your goals. As her accountability partner, I applaud Leslie for accomplishing her goals this past year.
—Sylathia Denise McCullough Johnson, My Sister

Accountability partners help keep us focused! In our busy lives, it is easy to procrastinate, forget, or even dismiss the very things we have set in place to keep us on track to reach our goals. Accountability partners, through their feedback, observation, and thought-provoking sincerity, help to get us where we want to be.
—Dr. Patti Copenny Reed, My Sorority Sister

An accountability partner is there to help you to stay balanced and true to your commitments. This person is a friend who gives you a different pair of eyes, is one who can be trusted, and has your best interest in the forefront always. They

encourage you, lift you, and in difficult moments, say words like "Girl, you got this!"
—Janet McCloud-Montgomery, My Sorority Sister

It is important to have people to encourage you because you need others to lift you up. You need a friend that you can believe in. It is important to encourage other people because that's why we are here. Your elders should see about you, offer fruitful thoughts, and make sure no negativity surrounds you whatsoever.
—Helen Guess Jones, My Aunt

Many people who did not accomplish a goal failed to do so because they did not have someone to hold them accountable to their commitment. It is important to have someone support and encourage you in life so that you do not feel lonely. I positively influence my mom because she gains perspective from another generation.
—Antasha J. Royal, My Daughter

It is important to have an accountability partner in my life because when I fall short of my goals, a good accountability partner is there to pick me up and offer encouraging words. It is important to have support because I might get off track, and I need that individual to put me back on track and tell me I can do it.
—Dr. Linda Williams Smith, My Friend

It is imperative to have accountability partners while pursuing goals to ensure that one remains focused on achieving goals even when the person may be facing obstacles.
—Lisa Kirk, My Best Friend (BFF)

It's important to have an accountability partner because that person will keep you on point, encourage you, and affirm you as a person continuously. I feel that my daughter Leslie has grown as a result of the women in this group. She has been excited this entire time. She is doing all the things on her list, such as taking care of her health with walking, exercising, and eating. I feel that Leslie, as my daughter, has become more engaging and continues to affirm me, uplift me as her mother, and treat me well at all times. She makes a point to spend more time with me and know all that is going on with me medically. I feel that I am spoiled by my daughter. She and Tony bring so much excitement to the lives of his mother and me. They take us on trips to different places and surprise us with fun things.
—Lizzie Dukes Guess, My Mother

It's good to have an accountability partner because oftentimes, you don't see yourself the way other people see you. It will give you a better outlook and perspective. You question things about yourself that you literally take for granted. You can bring those things you take for granted to the forefront. Motivation is a good thing always.
—Donna London, My Friend

Leslie E. Royal's Goals for 2015
Five Categories with Five Specific Areas of Focus
(Please find excerpts from my 2015 goals sent to my accountability partners. I updated them monthly. Create a list of goals that you would like to achieve. You can use my design or create your own.)

Spiritually Fit

1. Read the Bible in one year—Titled *Reading God's Story: A Chronological Daily Bible* by George H. Guthrie
2. Have thirty minutes to one hour of daily meditation and prayer
3. Call or visit church families requiring care and encouragement
4. Attend worship services regularly
5. Join in church corporate invocation via conference call weekly

Professionally Fit

I listed five specific career goals here. They related to my freelance writing career and Leslie's Lane, Inc.

1. Leslie's Lane Blog—_____
2. Leslie E. Royal freelance writing projects—_____
3. Earnings—_____
4. Leslie's Lane Projects—_____
5. Miscellaneous Projects—_____

Physically Fit

1. Complete two fitness challenges in 2015.
2. Weigh _____ pounds by December 31, 2015, through proper eating and exercise.
3. Read at least two books on healthy living
4. Do FREE or low-cost workout five days a week
5. Drink eight to ten glasses of water per day

Emotionally Fit

1. Watch TV shows just for fun!
2. Keep the fire going! (1) Have date night with my husband once a week! (2) Surprise him with something special once a month (3) Have a retreat with my husband every quarter
3. Bond with my children: (1) Monthly mother-daughter dinner and (2) Monthly mother-son luncheon
4. Contact and care for my family and friends on a regular basis
5. Have ALL CASH travel or day trips with family on quarterly basis

Financially Fit

1. Continue to make a budget and stick to it! Tell that dollar where to go!
2. Continue to pay my tithes
3. Continue to save/invest
4. Continue to save for emergency reserve fund
5. Allocate the remaining funds to household expenses and discretionary expenditures

Next, it's always cool to have mentors and to network. It's a great idea to be part of a group of like-minded individuals in the same career or who have the passion that you have! I am actually a member of a private Facebook group called International Media Ladies (IML). By way of background, my daughter Antasha and I went to St. Croix on a press trip. The photo above is of us on the outside of the beautiful Renaissance St. Croix Carambola Beach Resort & Spa just after a great breakfast! We met so many wonderful journalists! We all con-nected so well that we decided to create this great group! I asked a few of them to share the importance of connecting with other like-minded individuals.

It is so important to have a network of like-minded individuals striving for excellence. They are tasked with keeping you from falling. If you fall, they are right there to catch you. The network is there to keep you lifted, encouraged, and supported at all times. It has a connection to your final product and can help you with your vision of getting where you want to be.
—Janet McCloud Montgomery, member of IML
and Creator of From My Big Eyes Blog

Leslie mentioned in an e-mail that said, "Iron sharpens iron." Mutual and genuine support, feedback, and networking provide the steady framework for progress—toward revealing the limitless gifts that each person has to offer.
—Kimberly J. Hamilton-Wright,
Member of IML and Freelance Journalist

Leslie E. Royal

It is so true iron sharpens iron. Like-minded individuals push you, encourage you, and bring out the best in you. They challenge you to see things from different angles and sometimes push you out of your comfort zone. Sharing new ideas and processes helps all to grow!
—Brenda Washington O'Neale,
Member of IML and Creator of With This Ring Travel Blog

As you pursue your passion and create the job of your dreams, try creating a vision board! Here are a few more tips from my blog posting earlier this year!

January 2016 Leslie's Lane: The Gift of 2016! A Vision of a Promising New Year and Fearless New You!

Posted on January 24, 2016, by Leslie's Lane

Hi, Beautiful Family and Friends!

How are you? I trust that you doing well! It's a New Year and it brings much promise! For the first time ever, I created a Vision Board. I had heard about them and even wrote briefly about this concept in one of my past postings. My pastor, Dr. Kerwin B. Lee of Berean Christian Church, hosted an awesome Vision Board Party. My wonderful hubby Tony, my children Tasha and Jay, and I attended. It was so cool! I decided to use January Leslie's Lane to share a little about how the theme of my vision board unfolded. I trust that this month's posting is helpful as you prepare for an amazing year! Thanks so much; have a great week!

Sincerely,

Leslie E. Royal

1. **Write the vision.** My vision for 2016 is to understand "The Gift" in my life and harness the amazing power therein. So after much prayer and meditation, I realized the theme of my Vision Board would be "The Gift"!

If you would like to create a Vision Board this year, click on this link for plenty of great info: https://www.google.com/search?q=write+the+vision+and+make+it+plain&oq=write+the+vision+and+make+&aqs=chrome.0.0j69i57j0l4.6498j0j4&sourceid=chrome&es_sm=122&ie=UTF-8#q=how+to+make+a+vision+board

2. **What's the theme for 2016?** Everything in my life centers around my faith. Romans 6:23b shares, "The gift of God is eternal life in Christ Jesus our Lord." In the center of my board, I created a gift design of silver ribbons with a silver bow in the center. It is also a cross. Looking at the board daily, I am reminded that this New Year is a wonderful gift of life, and I look forward to enjoying it abundantly. What is your theme for 2016 and how will you live it out?

3. **Follow your dreams with boldness.** That's my motto for this year! I have several special projects in mind! I want to pursue my passion! As such, I clipped out all kinds of words from magazines that would encourage me to do so! Trigger words to get me moving are FEARLESS NOW, Dream Big, Year of You, Do It, Turn It Up, ACTION, Unstoppable, and more! What buzzwords or triggers will spur you to action in 2016? What have you always wanted to do? If you want to start your own business, check out this link: http://www.essence.com/2015/02/23/sister-ceo-7-great-tips-starting-your-own-company-year. What about that raise you've been wanting? Here's how to ask for it: http://fortune.com/2015/03/03/get-the-raise-you-deserve/.

4. **Focusing on family, fitness, and fun.** My family is a priority in my life! No question about it! I especially enjoy spending time with my hubby, children, mom, sisters, brother, godchildren, and extended family members! We take part in really cool fitness challenges, and enjoy taking vacations at great discounts! You have to relax, unwind, and kick back sometime! What do you like to do for fun? Check out a few of my favorite search engines to help you out with attractions, hotels, transportation, restaurants, and more! They are TripAdvisor, Expedia and Google Flights! Check out this link too: https://www.

google.com/search?q=vacations+leslie+c+royal&oq=vacations+le
slie+e+royal&aqs=chrome..69i57.10544j0j4&sourceid=chrome
&es_sm=122&ie=UTF-8.

5. **What is uniquely you?** No two vision boards are the same, because no two people are the same! Your vision board will reflect your beautiful, creative, distinct personality! For example, I made my board in 3-D because I am multidimensional! I see things from a number of different perspectives!! While some vision boards have lots of space on them, mine is completely full! That's because I want to experience every single moment of life! I use every minute of the day! While my board appears to be compartmentalized in four distinct areas of faith (church), family, finance (work/career), and fun (travel), I have a cross and my family in every section! That's because my faith guides me in all that I do, and my family is a part of all that I do! What is unique about you, and how are you going to share it with the world in 2016? Your time is NOW! Seize the MOMENT!

If you have a vision for starting your own business, check out an article that I wrote for *ESSENCE* that you will find quite helpful: http://www.essence.com/2015/02/23/sister-ceo-7-great-tips-starting-your-own-company-year

Are you interested in federal government contracts? Check out these sites:
www.sba.gov/contracting
www.fedbizopps.gov
www.sam.gov

To learn more about federal grants, check out www.grants.gov. They cover agriculture, cultural affairs, community development, environment, energy, health, law, science, technology, and more.

How about "300 Awesome FREE Things"? I love this comprehensive list created by Ali Mese! It will be quite helpful as you get your business off the ground. If you have scarce resources, take advantage of FREE stuff such as free websites, social media resources, design and code, stock photography, startup info, free typography, remote work, surveys, and so much more. http://thenextweb.com/dd/2015/02/18/300-awesome-free-things-massive-list-free-resources-know/#gref

When I decided to create my Leslie's Lane website, I settled on Go Daddy. I liked all of the resources that it offered at an affordable price. I signed on to the .99 cents domain deal they were offering at the time. Check out this link if you are interested in their site: https://www.godaddy.com/. Also, Google Go Daddy .99 cents to find out about this offer.

Five ways to get the raise you deserve: http://fortune.com/2015/03/03/get-the-raise-you-deserve/

Protect your script or television show idea! Have you come up with a great idea for a television show? Have you written a script? Protect it for a minimal cost with the Writer's Guild of America. Check out these links for East or West: https://www.wgaeast.org/script_registration?gclid=CPyQlJSK2sECFVNk7A odUnUAhw
https://www.wgawregistry.org/webrss/

Ready to live your dreams as an actor or actress? All people should chase their dreams with intensity and pursue their passion! Why not start TODAY? Check out these auditions and casting calls!
http://www.backstage.com/
www.actorsaccess.com
www.actorsequity.org
www.playbill.com
www.nowcasting.com
www.starnow.com
www.castnet.com

To learn about many, many franchises, check out this link: http://www.franchisedirect.com.

Do you take photos just for fun? Well…why not sell them? Here are some great websites to sell your photos:
Photoshelter—http://www.photoshelter.com/
Dreamstime—https://www.dreamstime.com/
Shutterstock—http://www.shutterstock.com/
Fotolia—www.fotolia.com
iStockphoto—http://www.istockphoto.com/
Snapped4U—http://snapped4u.com/
Can Stock Photo—www.canstockphoto
Fotola—www.fotola.com

Look Who's Thirty and Ready to Go on the Ride of a Lifetime!
In the photo above, I was celebrating my thirtieth birthday! I was so happy in that moment! Yet…. I was more than a little nervous and fearful. I had just turned thirty, quit my secure job at the FBI and cut off all my hair!!!! I decided to follow my dream of being a full-time freelance writer! The gentleman looking on in the picture was Mr. David Smith. He was my first editor and publisher. Just two years prior, with a little help from my daughter Antasha, I had an epiphany. I realized that I should focus on my passion.

I pulled out the yellow pages and called every single newspaper and magazine in Atlanta. No one would hire me. They all said, "You need experience." But about a week later, Mr. Smith of the *Atlanta Bulletin* newspaper called me back. He said, "Mrs. Royal, I will be glad to have you. I don't pay my writers. But you can write for me and gain experience. You can take that experience and go on to write for other publications." His words could not have been more profound. Mr. Smith passed away in 1998. But I will always remember him as a great editor, publisher, boss, mentor, counselor, and friend. I wrote for the *Atlanta Bulletin* for two years before I resigned from the FBI.

I soon began writing for Jennifer Parker of *CrossRoadsNews*—http://crossroadsnews.com/ She paid me my first fifty dollars as a writer! I cashed that check and placed the first one-dollar bill handed to me in a small compartment in my wallet. I intended to frame it the way most people do. But I never got around to it. I have been carrying it around in my wallet for years! I've changed wallets several times, but I simply move the one-dollar bill along with other contents. If you are ready to follow your dream as a writer, check out my blog post below:

So You Want to Be a Writer? Check Out These Ten FREELANCE WRITING WEBSITES and RESOURCES!

https://leslieslane.wordpress.com/2016/02/02/so-you-want-to-be-a-writer-check-out-these-10-freelance-writing-websites-and-resources/

Posted on February 2, 2016, by Leslie's Lane

Hi, Beautiful Family and Friends!
How are you? I trust that you are having a great day! I wanted to share some great info with you! As many of you know, I have been a freelance writer for more than twenty years! It is my passion, and I LOVE doing it! Well…recently, a friend of mine, Joia Ellis-Dinkins, the branch manager of Georgia Hill Library in Atlanta, Georgia, invited me to come out to speak! I spoke on the subject: "Learn How to Get Published in a Magazine, Newspaper, or Online Source." I really had a great time, and the attendees were wonderful! For those of you who are aspiring writers, I decided to share a little info with you! I trust that you find it helpful! Thanks so much, and have a wonderful week!

Ten Great Freelance Writing Websites and Resources

1. Contena is a website offering comprehensive job postings.
   https://www.contena.co/

2. Eight websites to start your freelance writing career:
   http://www.shoutmeloud.com/8-websites-to-start-your-freelance-writing-career.html

3. "20 great websites for freelance writers"
   https://www.flexjobs.com/blog/post/20-great-websites-for-freelance-writers/

4. Freelancewriting.com has a database of more than 818 writer's guidelines.
   http://www.freelancewriting.com/guidelines/pages/

5. Magazines that publish short stories, essays, and poems:
   http://www.everywritersresource.com/topliterarymagazines.html

6. Forty-six literary magazines for short stories:
   http://letswriteashortstory.com/literary-magazines/

7. Twenty-three magazines and websites that want your short story:
   http://thewritelife.com/where-to-submit-short-stories/

8. The one hundred most popular magazines in the United States:
   http://www.listchallenges.com/100-most-popular-magazines-in-the-us

9. How to find press trips for travel writers:
   http://www.pitchtravelwrite.com/press-trips-for-travel-writers.html

10. Freelance Writing Jobs: 25 Sites That Pay for Guest Posts
    http://www.aol.com/article/2015/01/24/sites-buy-guest-posts/21132908/?gen=1

Leslie's Listening!
OK…let's talk! I wanted this book to be interactive. I would love to partner with you as you become inspired, empowered, and informed. Here are a few questions for you to consider as you ponder what you want from this chapter.

If money were no factor and you could have the job of your dreams, what would it be?

_____
_____

How are you going to start working on your dream?

_____
_____

Do you want to start your own business?

_____
_____

What would it be, and what would you offer?

_____
_____

What resources do you need to succeed?

_____
_____

Is there anything that I have not asked that you would like to share?

_____
_____
_____
_____
_____

OK! Let's get to WORK!

Nine

Social Media

Greetings, Beautiful Friends! ☺

Let's face it! If we want to have a successful business, we have to be wired into social media! If we want to know what our kids are doing and stay connected to family and friends, we have to be on social media. If we want up-to-date, minute-by-minute information on what's going on in the world, we must be a part of social media.

I have found social media to be an essential and invaluable tool in sharing important information about Leslie's Lane. I know I mentioned it earlier in the introduction, but a friendly reminder: Please "Like" the Leslie's Lane Facebook page. Follow me on Twitter and Instagram @LesliesLane. Sign up for Leslie's Lane information by going to my website at http://www.leslieslane.com/. And check out my blog site called www.LesliesLane.wordpress.com.

At the end of this chapter, feel free to query yourself to find out which social media sites and various aspects of them would work best for you! Thanks so much for your support, and have a great week! Happy Reading and Research!

Sincerely,

Leslie

Can you tell me about social media?

"I would like to learn most about how to make myself more marketable in my work on social media sites like LinkedIn. Projects that I am currently interested in are the recent relief efforts concentrated on my hometown area in West Virginia. I grew up in Pinch, West Virginia. Recently, areas around my hometown experienced great loss with recent large-scale flooding. There are several efforts on social media such as Facebook and Twitter that have orchestrated gathering cleaning supplies, water, clothing, and personal hygiene products for the victims of the flooding. Social media is always changing. I always look forward to learning what they will come up with next. Can you tell me about promoting myself and projects on social media?"

— *Ginnie Kate Oglesby is a registered nurse and wants to use social media to serve neighbors and hone her professional skills.*

Perspective & Words of Advice
from *Leslie's Lane: The Book!*
Social Media Expert

"The community on LinkedIn is comprised of business owners or career professionals specifically looking to connect and network for mutually beneficial arrangements. Each user has a clear goal and they log in to the site to take specific action versus spending hours browsing like Facebook users do. The key to attracting clients online is to build your online platform so that anytime you show up online, you are not wasting time. A social media update could lead to new business, but if you don't have a clear strategy for those postings, then you're just wasting time. If you want to promote your business, currently, one of the best places is Facebook and in particular Facebook Live. Video provides business owners with a high-impact, high-value piece of marketing material. And since Facebook has prioritized video, it's a great time to take advantage. If you are trying to promote social events, live streaming is a great way to promote special events because there is high engagement. Beyond that I would recommend creating an event on Facebook and boosting the event via an ad to your local area."

— *LaTisha Styles is the President of Financial Success Media, LLC,*

Leslie's Lessons—Five Tips at a Glance! Check Out Some of the Best Social Media Websites

1. www.facebook.com
2. www.twitter.com
3. www.instagram.com
4. www.linkedin.com
5. https://plus.google.com/

Leslie's Litany—Three Books to Read! Check Out Some of the Best Social Media Books

1. *500 Social Media Marketing Tips* by Andrew Macarthy
2. *Likeable Social Media* by Dave Kerpen
3. *Social Media Mastery* by Tara Ross

Leslie's Lane The Book!
Expert Info at a Glance!
Company: Financial Success Media LLC
Website: http://LaTishaStyles.com/
Facebook: http://facebook.com/latishatv
Twitter: http://twitter.com/LaTishaStylesTV
Instagram: http://instagram.com/LaTishaStylesTV

It's time to get interactive. The type of social media you use can depend upon what you want to achieve: just talk to friends, promote your business, and so forth. I love Facebook because I can stay connected to my family, friends, sorority sisters of Alpha Kappa Alpha Sorority, Inc., church members from Berean Christian Church, classmates from Savannah High School's class of '85, and more!

As in my case, if you are just getting your business off the ground, start with Hootsuite. Thanks to my friend Chinedu Agbaere, whom I affectionately call "Dr. Chin," I learned that this site manages your other sites simultaneously. So when I publish one post, it posts to Facebook, Twitter, Instagram, Google+, LinkedIn, WordPress, and more! How cool is that? Right now, I post to ten social media sites. In the months to come, I will be exploring all different types of social media sites as I expand the Leslie's Lane brand. Check out all these cool sites. Many are FREE!

Hootsuite—https://hootsuite.com/
Facebook—https://www.facebook.com/
Twitter—https://twitter.com/
Youtube—https://www.youtube.com/
Google+—https://plus.google.com/
Pinterest—https://www.pinterest.com/
LinkedIn—https://www.linkedin.com/
Vine—https://vine.co/
Instagram—https://www.instagram.com/
Snapchat—https://www.snapchat.com/
Tumblr—https://www.tumblr.com/dashboard
Swarm—https://www.swarmapp.com/
Reddit—https://www.reddit.com/
Periscope—https://www.periscope.tv/
Foursquare—https://foursquare.com/
Flickr—https://www.flickr.com/
Soundcloud—https://soundcloud.com/
Tinder—https://www.gotinder.com/

Peach—http://peach.cool/
Xing—https://www.xing.com/en
Renren—http://www.renren-inc.com/en/
Disqus—https://disqus.com/
YikYak—https://www.yikyak.com/home
Shots—https://shots.com/
Twoo—https://www.twoo.com/
Medium—https://medium.com/
Meetup—http://www.meetup.com/
WhatsApp—https://www.whatsapp.com/
Goodreads—https://www.goodreads.com/
SlackSocial—http://slacksocial.com/
Slack—https://slack.com/
Yelp—www.yelp.com
Musical.ly—http://musical.ly/
TravBuddy.com—http://www.travbuddy.com/
Blab—https://blab.im/
Line—http://line.me/en/
Kik Messenger—https://www.kik.com/
Omegle—http://www.omegle.com/

If you are trying to reach just the right audience, please check out my *ESSENCE* article: "Cyber Sister: Using Social Media to Reach Your Niche Audience for the Holidays" at http://www.essence.com/2015/11/24/cyber-sister-using-social-media-reach-your-niche-audience-holidays.

Leslie's Listening!

OK…let's talk! I wanted this book to be interactive. I would love to partner with you as you become inspired, empowered, and informed. Here are a few questions for you to consider as you ponder what you want from this chapter.

How would you like to use social media?

_____

_____

Do you have a business? If so, how do you need to market it?

_____

_____

Do you want to get to know others better socially?

_____

_____

How do you intend to do so on social media?

_____

_____

Want to keep up with friends and family on social media?

_____

_____

Is there anything that I have not asked that you would like to share?

_____

_____

_____

_____

OK! Let's get to WORK!

Ten

HEART AND SOUL: SERVING HUMANITY

Greetings, Beautiful Friends! ☺

As a woman of faith, I am bound by a covenant of serving others. It is also vitally important to me to live my life fully and completely. It is important to me to do so by serving my community in tangible ways. In Oprah Winfrey's words, I want to "live my best life!" What is your "best life"? What do you want most out of life? What would make your life complete? It may take a great deal of introspection, but you've got what it takes to figure it out.

It is just so important to me to serve, inspire, empower, educate, and motivate others! That's what Leslie's Lane is all about! I believe that virtually all faiths throughout the world share a common bond and thread, that is, our mutual desire and commitment to serve humanity.

If you are searching for meaning in your life, and would like to serve humanity in tangible ways, peruse the information in this chapter to find organizations and programs to help others. At the end, you can meditate on the questions. Thanks so much for your support, and have a great week! Happy Reading and Research!

Sincerely,

Leslie

Can you tell me about serving humanity?

"I have gone on mission trips to Honduras and volunteered with churches, museums, schools and the Boy Scouts. I feel we have a responsibility to make the world a better place. How do I know if a mission trip is right for me? What opportunities currently exist to serve humanity? How do I contact the organizations?"

— *C. David Moody, Jr, a successful businessman, is the founder and CEO of C. D. Moody Construction Company, Inc. He wants to know more about serving his community.*

Perspective & Words of Advice
from *Leslie's Lane: The Book!*
Serving Humanity Experts

"Some of the benefits of serving others are positively impacting their lives holistically and empowering them to make better decisions in life that lead to their success. Contact nonprofit organizations within the area (churches, YMCA, YWCA, Boys and Girls Clubs and shelters) and find out what they are in need of and how one can volunteer with them. Opportunities for mission work help participants make a positive difference in the lives of individuals who desperately need a hand out and up. Two great ways to find out about mission trips are by word of mouth and the internet."

— *Dr. Kerwin B. Lee is the Senior Pastor of Berean Christian Church. Having three locations, the organization is committed to local and international missions.*

"We serve humanity by encouraging faith, hope and love. Social media has changed the way we communicate. There is so much information at our disposal. Most churches, companies, agencies and schools maintain more than one social media platform. So, by liking, following, retweeting and sharing social media posts from and about your local community, an individual is bound to be inundated with opportunities to serve."

— *Dr. James Flanagan is the President of Luther Rice College & Seminary – an institution named for a globally renowned minister and missionary.*

"Serving humanity is our reason for being. I founded Forty Days to Deliverance to empower men and to help them discover their purpose. If you have a desire to serve humanity and are searching for meaning in your life, try serving in different areas in your community until you find what is fulfilling for you. Start by using Google to search faith-based organizations in your area, governmental organizations like The Peace Corps and global initiatives such as Care International."

— *Tony Royal is the Founder of a new nonprofit organization called Forty Days to Deliverance.*

Leslie's Lessons—Five Tips at a Glance! Check Out Some of the Heart and Soul Websites

1. http://www.peacecorps.gov/volunteer/
2. https://www.habitat.org
3. http://www.care-international.org/
4. http://experiencemission.org/
5. http://www.reachmissiontrips.org/

Leslie's Litany—Three Books to Read! Check Out Some of the Best Heart and Soul Books

1. *Cross-Cultural Servanthood* by Duane Elmer
2. *Chicken Soup for the Soul: Volunteering and Giving Back* by Amy Newmark and Carrie Morgridge
3. *The Generosity Factor: The Joy of Giving Your Time, Talent and Treasure* by Ken Blanchard and S. Truett Cathy

Leslie's Lane The Book!
Expert Info at a Glance!
Organization: Luther Rice College & Seminary
Website: http://www.lutherrice.edu/
Facebook: https://www.facebook.com/SeminaryOnline
Twitter: @Luther_Rice
Instagram: luther_rice

Leslie's Lane The Book!
Expert Info at a Glance!
Organization: Berean Christian Church
Website: www.bereanchristianchurch.org
Facebook: https://www.facebook.com/bereanchristianchurch
Twitter: @berean_cc
Instagram: @bereanchristianchurch

While reading the previous chapters, you may have noticed that with the exception of one, all have one expert. With this chapter, there are three gentlemen whom I admire deeply. I wanted to include each in this chapter on Heart and Soul. That's because they have spent their lives in service to others.

My pastor, Dr. Kerwin B. Lee, has a heart for serving others. The exceptional community initiatives that he implements empowers and impacts the entire region. Dr. James L. Flanagan, a humble man of excellence, is known for great deeds at Luther Rice College and Seminary and throughout the country. Actually, Dr. Lee and Dr. Flanagan impact the world globally with their respective organizations' service to humanity.

Since he was a young man, my dear husband, Tony Royal, has always cared for and served others. He did so throughout his more than thirty-five-year career in the quick service restaurant industry at KFC, Mrs. Winners, and Chick-fil-A. His family, friends and employees often referred others to him for counseling and resources.

As a Chick-fil-A Owner/Operator for sixteen years, Tony served his community in many ways. He loves the awesome Chick-fil-A company! It was an honor to work with its legendary founder S. Truett Cathy and the Cathy family. Talk about Heart & Soul, Truett was a true inspiration to all who met him. He authored several books which serve as great resources for those wanting to serve and needing to be inspired. They include: *It's Easier to Succeed Than to Fail, How Did You Do It, Truett: A Recipe for Success, Eat Mor Chikin: Inspire More People, Wealth: Is It Worth It* and *It's Better to Build Boys Than to Mend Men.*

Oh yes! Everything wonderful you hear about the Chick-fil-A family and the Cathy family is true! They are the "salt of the earth," and it was a pleasure for us to be associated with them. But in 2000, Tony envisioned forming an organization that would empower men who are jobless or homeless and have simply lost their way. In July 2016, he made that vision a reality by founding Forty Days to Deliverance, a nonprofit organization, to help men discover their purpose in life.

C. David Moody is a successful businessman in the metro Atlanta community. He makes the *Black Enterprise* List every year: http://www.blackenterprise. com/lists/be-100s-2015/. I asked him to be a part of this chapter because I've noticed that not only has he given so much of himself and volunteers perpetually in his community, he is also always looking for different ways to serve.

Like Moody and countless others, would you like to serve others by volunteering in your community? In addition to the aforementioned books, *Make a Difference: America's Guide to Volunteering and Community Service*, by Arthur J. Blaustein, may be helpful to you. Further, many of the organizations below provide an opportunity to serve individuals who are most in need.

Boys and Girls Club of America http://www.bgca.org/
YMCA http://www.ymca.net/volunteer/
YWCA http://www.ywca.org/
Rotary International https://www.rotary.org/
Kiwanis International http://www.kiwanis.org/
Cross Cultural Solutions https://www.crossculturalsolutions.org/
Volunteer Match http://www.volunteermatch.org/nonprofits/
Idealist http://www.idealist.org/
Bridge Span http://www.bridgespan.org/
Super Service Challenge https://superservicechallenge.com
Education Pioneers http://www.educationpioneers.org/
Mission Discovery http://www.missiondiscovery.org
Mission Finder https://missionfinder.org
The King Center http://www.thekingcenter.org/volunteer
The Enchanted Closet http://enchantedcloset.org/
Jobs for Life http://www.jobsforlife.org/
Children's Museum of Atlanta http://childrensmuseumatlanta.org/about-us/join-our-team/
GEEARS http://geears.org/ Operation Shoebox http://www.operationshoebox.com/volunteer-2/
Refuge Pregnancy Center http://refugepregnancycenter.com/Volunteer.htm

A Testimonial on Volunteering and Serving One's Community
"I volunteer at Refuge Pregnancy Center doing ultrasounds
for clients and teaching breastfeeding classes to new moms.
I enjoy seeking out information about serving. I really love
to serve in my community. I enjoy helping my children serve

in our community as well. Taking advantage of serving in our community has provided our family with many ways to develop character qualities such as servanthood, humility, thankfulness, and preferring others above yourself. I enjoy serving humanity by using my gifts and talents to help others. It is a really beautiful thing, and it brings much joy into my life. I am always looking for new places to serve. Some of the missions and nonprofit organizations I have worked in over the years are Operation Shoe Box, Open Door Mission to the homeless, and Refuge Pregnancy Center. I just want to add that volunteering in the community is a very rewarding endeavor. It is truly better to give than receive, and the greatest is the servant. If all of us join together to love and serve the needy in our communities, the world can become a better and more caring place."

—Candace Driskell, a home manager of twenty-two years, enjoys serving her community

A Testimonial on Volunteering and Serving One's Community

"Serving one's community is important to me because of the tremendous impact we can have by positively contributing to the lives of others. As the daughter of a minister and public servant and as the proud wife of a public servant, community service has been a part of who I am from the very beginning. I am proud to volunteer and be involved with organizations focusing on issues that I am passionate about. That includes The Children's Museum of Atlanta (inspiring children to learn through play), Georgia Early Education Alliance for Ready Students (providing statewide leadership on children's early learning and healthy development), and the nonprofit BiH (encouraging young people to pursue and fulfill their dreams). By serving others and volunteering, the community is strengthened and lives are often saved, changed and uplifted."

- Sarah-Elizabeth Langford Reed, First Lady, City of Atlanta

Leslie's Lane The Book!
Expert Info at a Glance!
Organization: Forty Days to Deliverance
Website: http://www.fortydaystodeliverance.com/
Facebook: https://www.facebook.com/FortyDaysToDeliverance
Twitter: @40DaysToDeliver
Instagram: @FortyDaysToDeliverance

How to Create Your Own Nonprofit Organization to Serve Others

Do you feel there is a void in your community that needs to be filled? Do you have a heart for serving others? My husband Tony has had that giving and serving heart since he was a youth. Before I give info on how to form your own nonprofit, a few of the leaders that have worked with Tony for years share what they think of his heart for serving others.

"He doesn't just care about you right now. He wants to make sure your tomorrow is secure spiritually, financially and in all ways."
– Kimberly Morris-Brown

"He serves others without expecting any reward or personal gain. He is loving, caring and inspiring."
– Cheryl Scott

"He has a heart of love, giving and kindness."
– Tawanna Bembry

"He doesn't judge a person by how they look or a disability. He gives others a chance when no one else will."
– Serena Gatson

"He has mentored myself and many others. I have witnessed him physically serving guests at the restaurant regardless of his executive status. Service is part of his very being."
– Chantel Toson

If you, like my husband Tony, are considering forming a new nonprofit, for starters, do this trilogy of things:

1. Create Your Name—https://www.sba.gov/starting-business/choose-register-your-business
2. Incorporate/register the organization—https://www.sba.gov/starting-business/choose-register-your-business/register-state-agencies
3. File for tax-exempt status—https://www.irs.gov/charities-non-profits/applying-for-tax-exempt-status

Then, check out these Small Business Association (SBA) sites and others:
https://www.sba.gov/tools/local-assistance
https://www.sba.gov/blogs/nonprofit-success-depends-your-business-mindset
www.grants.gov https://www.sba.gov/loans-grants/see-what-sba-offers/sba-loan-programs
https://www.sba.gov/blogs/could-you-finance-your-start-microloan
http://grantspace.org/tools/knowledge-base/Nonprofit-Management/Establishment/starting-a-nonprofit

There are numerous opportunities to share your wonderful talents by serving in your community. The organizations that I've listed so far are just a fraction of them. There is an old adage that I have heard since I was a little girl. That is, "God broke the mold when he made you," or "God broke the mold when he made me." What that meant is that particular person mentioned at that moment is a unique creation. You know, that's true of you. You are unique. You are different. You have distinctive, matchless, exceptional, unrivaled, and unparalleled talents that are your own. That means YOU ARE SPECIAL! YOU ARE A GIFT! Why not share the "GIFT of your SERVICE" with the world?

Leslie's Listening!

OK…let's talk! I wanted this book to be interactive. I would love to partner with you as you become inspired, empowered, and informed. Here are a few questions for you to consider as you ponder what you want from this chapter.

What do you most want out of life?

_____

_____

What do you think will complete you?

_____

_____

Why is it important to serve others?

_____

_____

Do you feel like you are blessed to be a blessing?

_____

_____

How are you paying it forward?

_____

_____

Is there anything that I have not asked that you would like to share?

_____

_____

_____

_____

OK! Let's get to WORK!

About the Author

Leslie E. Royal is the creator of Leslie's Lane—a consumer information blog. It is designed to be informational, educational, and inspirational. Her blog provides practical assistance in the area of jobs, discounts, free stuff, scholarships, internships, travel, and a wealth of other information that individuals find helpful in their daily lives.

Additionally, she has been a professional freelance writer for more than twenty years. She has written for many publications and online resources over her career. Presently, she writes for *ESSENCE, Business Accelerator/Dream Fearlessly, ESSENCE.com, UPSCALE,* and other media outlets. Her articles have included cover features as well as articles on parenting, business, consumer, Christianity, history, travel, arts, and high-profile celebrity interviews.

Leslie is a member of Berean Christian Church in Stone Mountain, Georgia, and serves in the Deacons Ministry. She is a member of the Authors Guild. Leslie is also a member of Alpha Kappa Alpha Sorority, Inc., Lambda Epsilon Omega Chapter, and its Forever Pink Foundation, Inc.

She holds a Bachelor of Arts Degree in Journalism from Georgia State University as well as a Master of Arts Degree in Christian Studies and Master of Divinity from Luther Rice College and Seminary. She and Tony have two adult children—Antasha and Jay.

Check Out Leslie's Lane Blog: Jobs, FREE Stuff, Discounts, Resources & More!
https://leslieslane.wordpress.com/
Check out her website at www.LesliesLane.com
Follow her on Twitter and Instagram @LesliesLane
Please check out her Facebook Page for info on Jobs, Discounts, FREE Stuff, Resources & More
https://www.facebook.com/LesliesLaneFREEStuff

Mr. David Smith
My Very First Editor and Publisher

It was not until five years after receiving my Bachelor of Arts degree in Journalism that I actually attempted to use it. I called numerous publications, and they would not accept me. That is until I contacted David Smith, the publisher of the *Atlanta Bulletin* newspaper. Because he gave me an opportunity when no one else would, he and his lovely wife, Joann, will always be in my heart. Though Mr. Smith has passed on, I feel his life's work lives on in me and his former writers.

Editors' Notes!

"For years, Leslie has ferreted information about everything, from job vacancies to great free stuff and free things to do, and shared it with her 'Beautiful Family and Friends' in her Leslie's Lane blog. A competent and caring writer, she understands the power of the written word, and uses it well to educate and inform her readers."

Jennifer Parker
Editor/Publisher, *CrossRoadsNews*, the first publication to pay Leslie for writing

"Fresh and engaging. These are two words I often used to describe the work in words that Leslie completed for say amen *more than a decade ago. I'm delighted to see that she's continued and elevated her craft with the Leslie's Lane blog. It makes me want to pack my bags and explore!"*

Faye Jackson Shannon
CEO/Marketing Wizard, vide, Inc. and Leslie's former Publisher at *say amen* magazine

"Leslie and I met in the late 1990s as editors at UPSCALE, where we shared an office. God-given joy and kindness, the unconditional gift of sharing tools for progress, the insatiable urgency to encourage others toward pursuing their

potential, and excellence in writing are just several of Leslie's numerous and wonderful qualities. Leslie's Lane embodies her relentless spirit to arm others with current, helpful information, and inspiration for advancement."

Kimberly J. Hamilton
Writer, freelance journalist, and Leslie's former lifestyle editor at UPSCALE magazine as well as former "officemate" when Leslie was an assignment editor at the publication

"When Leslie first introduced Leslie's Lane, I thought it was an excellent idea. Leslie's genuine passion for helping the community shines as she gives the scoop on where to find jobs, get free stuff, and travel on a dime. If you want good info from a trusted resource, read Leslie's Lane."

Tanisha A. Sykes
Leslie's former consumer affairs editor at Black Enterprise magazine and her former senior editor of personal finance and careers at ESSENCE magazine

Leslie's Library of Links

Check out a few of Leslie's Litany of articles over the past twenty years!

FORTUNE.COM
http://fortune.com/2015/03/03/get-the-raise-you-deserve/

ESSENCE **and ESSENCE.com**
http://www.essence.com/2016/01/15/sorority-power
http://www.essence.com/2015/12/17/5-unique-black-women-owned-ven-ues-your-last-minute-holiday-soiree
http://www.essence.com/2015/12/03/shop-purpose-how-one-woman-man-aged-buyblack-year
http://www.essence.com/2015/11/24/cyber-sister-using-social-media-reach-your-niche-audience-holidays
http://www.essence.com/2015/11/15/it%E2%80%99s-sister-thing-impor-tance-shopping-black-womens-businesses-season
http://www.essence.com/galleries/buyblack-essence-list-89-black-owned-businesses-shop-holidays
http://www.essence.com/2015/10/17/let%E2%80%99s-not-spend-much-money-christmas
http://www.essence.com/2014/11/14/shop-smart
http://www.essence.com/2014/04/13/how-gain-financial-freedom
http://www.essence.com/2015/02/23/sister-ceo-7-great-tips-starting-your-own-company-year http://www.essence.com/2015/02/23/5-great-ways-impress-your-boss-and-get-raise-you-deserve-2015
http://www.essence.com/2014/10/03/game-changers-power-list
http://www.essence.com/2015/01/01/join-2015-new-years-financial-revolu-tion
http://www.essence.com/2014/10/02/rising-stars-michelle-bernard/
http://www.essence.com/2014/10/02/rising-stars-charlene-dance
http://www.essence.com/2014/11/28/broke-blessed-how-earn-multiple-streams-income

http://www.essence.com/2014/11/12/broke-blessed-getting-out-credit-card-debt
http://www.essence.com/2014/10/27/broke-blessed
http://www.essence.com/2014/09/18/5-smart-answers-tough-interview-questions
http://www.essence.com/2014/09/11/social-media-and-your-career-change
http://www.essence.com/2015/01/29/broke-blessed-how-manage-your-student-loan-debt
http://www.essence.com/2015/01/29/broke-blessed-increase-your-credit-score

Chron.com
http://work.chron.com/build-oil-field-resume-27465.html
http://work.chron.com/revising-supervisor-do-27486.html
http://work.chron.com/become-christian-spiritual-retreat-director-28290.html
http://work.chron.com/copy-editor-career-outlook-26669.html

Black Enterprise
http://www.blackenterprise.com/mag/recovering-from-bank-fraud/
http://www.blackenterprise.com/lifestyle/airline-passenger-rights-updated/
http://www.blackenterprise.com/mag/5-situations-when-it%E2%80%99s-ok-to-close-a-credit-card/
http://www.blackenterprise.com/mag/how-to-prepare-for-an-audit/
http://www.blackenterprise.com/lifestyle/become-an-empowered-patient/
http://www.blackenterprise.com/lifestyle/summer-travel-deals/
http://www.blackenterprise.com/lifestyle/green-credit-cards/
http://www.blackenterprise.com/mag/5-ways-to-reduce-debt/
http://www.blackenterprise.com/mag/save-money-on-healthcare-costs/
http://www.blackenterprise.com/mag/5-ways-to-build-your-budget/
http://www.blackenterprise.com/mag/choosing-the-right-tax-professional/
http://www.blackenterprise.com/mag/true-colors/
http://www.blackenterprise.com/mag/flying-the-passenger-friendly-skies/

http://www.blackenterprise.com/mag/its-a-family-reunion/
http://www.blackenterprise.com/mag/an-apple-a-day/
http://www.blackenterprise.com/mag/its-a-new-year/
http://www.blackenterprise.com/mag/its-a-family-affair-7/
http://www.blackenterprise.com/mag/the-rap-doctor/
http://www.blackenterprise.com/mag/i-apologize/
http://www.blackenterprise.com/mag/its-a-family-affair-2/
http://www.blackenterprise.com/mag/living-the-glamorous-life/
http://www.blackenterprise.com/mag/the-perpetual-world-of-change/
http://www.blackenterprise.com/mag/when-it-rains-it-pours/
http://www.blackenterprise.com/mag/going-once-going-twice-2/
http://www.blackenterprise.com/mag/the-mysterious-underwriters/
http://www.blackenterprise.com/mag/want-to-lower-your-auto-insurance/
http://www.blackenterprise.com/mag/in-too-deep/
http://www.blackenterprise.com/mag/the-clock-is-ticking/
http://www.blackenterprise.com/mag/the-doctor-will-e-mail-you-now/
http://www.blackenterprise.com/mag/its-in-the-mail/
http://www.blackenterprise.com/mag/vacation-research-made-easy/
http://www.blackenterprise.com/mag/the-rising-cost-of-medicine/
http://www.blackenterprise.com/mag/lost-in-translation/
http://www.blackenterprise.com/mag/all-the-right-moves/
http://www.blackenterprise.com/mag/unjust-clause/
http://www.blackenterprise.com/mag/total-recall-2/
http://www.blackenterprise.com/mag/homeowners-associations/
http://www.blackenterprise.com/mag/sour-auto-power/
http://www.blackenterprise.com/mag/whats-the-411-2/
http://www.blackenterprise.com/mag/settle-for-lesswith-the-irs/
http://www.blackenterprise.com/mag/high-speed-web-access/
http://www.blackenterprise.com/mag/forgive-us-our-debts-%e2%80%a6/
http://www.blackenterprise.com/mag/from-dream-to-reality/
http://www.blackenterprise.com/mag/first-time-visit-to-a-resale-shop/
http://www.blackenterprise.com/mag/fair-credit-reporting-act-tweaked-by-congress/

http://www.blackenterprise.com/mag/across-the-border/
http://www.blackenterprise.com/mag/get-used-to-it/
http://www.blackenterprise.com/mag/legal-ease/
http://www.blackenterprise.com/mag/looting-luggage/
http://www.blackenterprise.com/mag/im-sorry-just-wont-do/
http://www.blackenterprise.com/mag/no-saving-grace/
http://www.blackenterprise.com/mag/home-free/
http://www.blackenterprise.com/mag/tightening-your-belt/
http://www.blackenterprise.com/mag/looks-like-a-bargain/
http://www.blackenterprise.com/mag/heated-about-your-gas-bill/
http://www.blackenterprise.com/mag/not-for-sale/
http://www.blackenterprise.com/mag/art-aids-africa/
http://www.blackenterprise.com/mag/creditors-in-your-closet/
http://www.blackenterprise.com/mag/whats-the-411/
http://www.blackenterprise.com/mag/creepin-credit-errors/
http://www.blackenterprise.com/mag/housing-bias-bust/
http://www.blackenterprise.com/mag/cable-connections/
http://www.blackenterprise.com/mag/when-diamonds-arent-forever/
http://www.blackenterprise.com/mag/all-inclusive-trips/
http://www.blackenterprise.com/mag/happy-kwanzaa/
http://www.blackenterprise.com/mag/top-10-reasons-to-dump-your-bank/
http://www.blackenterprise.com/mag/smart-credit-card-use/
http://www.blackenterprise.com/mag/save-time-and-money-on-the-net/
http://www.blackenterprise.com/mag/online-shoppers-beware/
http://www.blackenterprise.com/mag/consumer-information-catalog/
http://www.blackenterprise.com/mag/debt-free-is-the-way-to-be/
http://www.blackenterprise.com/mag/consumer-information-catalog/
http://www.blackenterprise.com/mag/free-online-surfing/
http://www.blackenterprise.com/mag/email-travel-savings/
http://www.blackenterprise.com/mag/cut-your-mortgage-cost/
http://www.blackenterprise.com/mag/free-money/
http://www.blackenterprise.com/mag/reap-the-rebates/

http://www.blackenterprise.com/mag/home-buying-101/
http://www.blackenterprise.com/mag/a-presidential-touch/
http://www.blackenterprise.com/mag/hip-hop-on-top/

Acknowledgments

Thanks for Helping Create *Leslie's Lane The Book!*

Michael Angelo Chester—Photographer and Creative Designer

Born in Columbus, Georgia, and raised in Detroit, Michigan, Michael is a "visualist" whose career spans several decades. His exceptional work includes visual media, fine art, graphic art, still photography, and film/video. Michael obtained his degree in graphic arts from the Computer Arts Institute in San Francisco. He has designed CD covers, books, logos, and magazine ads for numerous clients. He created this book's cover image, designed the Q&A pages featuring the experts and Leslie's Line graphic, and served as Leslie's photographer for several photos.

Sheryl Nance Nash—Copy Editor

Sheryl Nance-Nash is a freelance journalist based in New York City. She specializes in personal finance, small business, travel, and career topics. Her work has appeared in *Money* magazine, the *New York Times, Newsday, Black Enterprise, Upscale, ABCNews.com, Forbes.com, Orbitz.com, travel.usnews.com, Essence, DailyFinance.com, AARP. org,* the *Tennessean,* and many others. She was this book's preliminary copy editor.

Donna London and Stephanie Janelle Bryant – Hair Stylists

A dynamic mother-daughter tandem, Donna London and Stephanie Janelle Bryant are Leslie's longtime hairstylists, mentors, and friends. They are the co-owners of Don Janelle Hair Salon. They were the hairstylists for all of Leslie's photo shoots as well as all the casual photos in this book. They specialize in trendy cuts and styles, relaxers, natural hair care, eyelashes, glamour makeup, master hair weaving, hair replacement, and lace front weaves. They also feature hair coloring that is specially designed for the client. Leslie's vibrant hair color is called "Leslie Red."

Photo credit: The Royal family photo on the dedication page was used with permission. ©Lifetouch, Inc. *Photography for a Lifetime. Photo taken at JCPenney Stonecrest studio.*

Contributors to *Leslie's Lane The Book!*
Special thanks to all my family, friends, and experts who contributed to my first book! Your love, counsel, friendship, and support mean so much! Thank you!

ABOVE ALL, I AM THANKFUL TO MY CREATOR!

Sincerely,

Leslie E. Royal